D1542225

To my brothers
Robert Clifford Peale, M.D., F.I.C.S.
&
The Reverend Leonard Delaney Peale
Effective Helpers of Mankind

NORMAN VINCENT PEALE

THE POWER

of

positive thinking

especially condensed for
this Gift Edition

DESIGNED BY GENE GALASSO

THE C. R. GIBSON COMPANY
NORWALK CONNECTICUT

❧

Acknowledgement is made to
FOUNDATION FOR CHRISTIAN LIVING
Pawling, New York
for permission to reprint certain excerpts from
"Self-Improvement Handbook,"
"What's Your Trouble?"
and the
"How Card" series
by Norman Vincent Peale.

❧

Copyright 1952 by Prentice-Hall, Inc.
© Copyright 1956 by Prentice-Hall, Inc.
Englewood Cliffs, N. J.

❧

*All rights reserved, including the right to reproduce this
book, or any portions thereof, in any form, except for
the inclusion of brief quotations in a review.*

❧

LIBRARY OF CONGRESS CATALOG CARD NUMBER 52-10833
PRINTED IN THE UNITED STATES OF AMERICA
68640 — T

PREFACE
to this Gift Edition

This special gift edition, a condensation from the original, retains all of the basic concepts of a simple, workable philosophy for a way of life.

The principles the book teaches were learned the hard way by trial and error in my personal search. Having found answers to some of my own problems, I felt that a sharing of insights and experiences which helped me might also help others.

I found my own answers in Biblical teachings and in the writings of the great thinkers who dealt with the powers inherent in every personality. I have merely tried to describe those truths in the language and thought forms understandable to present-day people. The life to which this book is a witness is very wonderful. Indeed, while often hard, it is also full of joy and hope and victory. When anyone orders his life on the basis of true spiritual motivation and practice and learns to think not negatively but positively, amazing results are demonstrated.

The concepts advanced teach the cultivation of peace of mind, not as an escape from life, but a power center out of which comes driving energy for constructive living. They teach positive thinking, not as a means to power and riches, but as the practical application of faith to overcome defeat and to accomplish worthwhile creative values in life. They offer happiness to a person who achieves victory over himself and the difficult circumstances encountered in this world.

Contents

Introduction

1. Believe in Yourself / 1
2. A Peaceful Mind Generates Power / 8
3. How to Have Constant Energy / 14
4. Try Prayer Power / 20
5. How to Create Your Own Happiness / 26
6. Stop Fuming and Fretting / 31
7. Expect the Best and Get it / 37
8. I Don't Believe in Defeat / 45
9. How to Break the Worry Habit / 50
10. Power to Solve Personal Problems / 58
11. How to Use Faith in Healing / 62
12. When Vitality Sags, Try This Health Formula / 68
13. Inflow of New Thoughts Can Remake You / 73
14. Relax for Easy Power / 79
15. How to Get People to Like You / 86
16. Prescription for Heartache / 94
17. How to Draw upon That Higher Power / 102

Epilogue

What this book can do for you

This book is written to suggest techniques and to give examples which demonstrate that you do not need to be defeated by anything, that you can have peace of mind, improved health, and a never-ceasing flow of energy. Of this I have no doubt at all for I have watched countless persons learn and apply a system of simple procedures that has brought about the foregoing benefits in their lives.

Altogether too many people are defeated by the everyday problems of life. They go struggling, perhaps even whining, through their days with a sense of dull resentment at what they consider the "bad breaks" life has given them. In a sense there may be such a thing as "the breaks" in this life, but there is also a spirit and method by which we can control and even determine those breaks.

In saying this I certainly do not ignore or minimize the hardships and tragedies of the world, but neither do I allow them to dominate. You can permit obstacles to control your mind to the point where they are uppermost and thus become the dominating factors in your thought pattern. By learning how to cast them from the mind, by refusing to become mentally subservient to them, and by channeling spiritual power through your thoughts you can rise above obstacles which ordinarily might defeat you. You need be defeated only if you are willing to be. This book teaches you how to "will" not to be.

The purpose of this book is a very direct and simple one. It is written with the sole objective of helping the reader achieve a happy, satisfying, and worthwhile life. I thoroughly and enthusiastically believe in certain demonstrated and effective principles which, when practiced, produce a victorious life. My aim is to set them forth in this volume in a logical, simple, and understandable manner so that the reader feeling a sense of need, may learn a practical method by which he can build for himself, with God's help, the kind of life he deeply desires.

If you read this book thoughtfully, carefully absorbing its teachings, and if you will sincerely and persistently practice the principles and formulas set forth herein, you can experience an amazing improvement within yourself. Your relations with other people will improve. You will become a more popular, esteemed, and well-liked individual. By mastering these principles, you will enjoy a delightful new sense of well-being. You may attain a degree of health not hitherto known by you and experience a new and keen pleasure in living. You will become a person of greater usefulness and will wield an expanded influence.

I need not point out that the powerful principles contained herein are not my invention but are given to us by the greatest Teacher who ever lived and who still lives. This book teaches applied Christianity; a simple yet scientific system of practical techniques of successful living that works.

NORMAN VINCENT PEALE

THE POWER
of
positive *thinking*

❧ 1 ❧

Believe In Yourself

 Believe in yourself! Have faith in your abilities! Without a humble but reasonable confidence in your own powers you cannot be successful or happy. But with sound self-confidence you can succeed. A sense of inferiority and inadequacy interferes with the attainment of your hopes, but self-confidence leads to self-realization and successful achievement. Because of the importance of this mental attitude, this book will help you believe in yourself and release your inner powers.

It is appalling to realize the number of pathetic people who are hampered and made miserable by the malady popularly called the inferiority complex. But you need not suffer from this trouble. When proper steps are taken, it can be overcome. You can develop creative faith in yourself — faith that is justified.

The greatest secret for eliminating the inferiority complex, which is another term for deep and profound self-doubt, is to fill your mind to overflowing with faith. Develop a tremendous faith in God and that will give you a humble yet soundly realistic faith in yourself.

The acquiring of dynamic faith is accomplished by prayer, lots

1

of prayer, by reading and mentally absorbing the Bible and by practicing its faith techniques. In another chapter I deal with specific formulas of prayer, but I want to point out here that the type of prayer that produces the quality of faith required to eliminate inferiority is of a particular nature. Surface skimming, formalistic and perfunctory prayer is not sufficiently powerful.

Roland Hayes, the singer, quoted his grandfather to me, a man whose education was not equal to that of his grandson, but whose native wisdom was obviously sound. He said, "The trouble with lots of prayers is they ain't got no suction." Drive your prayers deep into your doubts, fears, inferiorities. Pray deep, big prayers that have plenty of suction and you will come up with powerful and vital faith.

Go to a competent spiritual adviser and let him teach you how to have faith. The ability to possess and utilize faith and gain the release of powers it provides are skills and, like any skills, must be studied and practiced to gain perfection.

At the conclusion of this chapter are listed ten suggestions for overcoming your inferiority pattern and for developing faith. Practice these rules diligently and they will aid you in developing confidence in yourself by dissipating your feelings of inferiority, however deeply imbedded.

At this point, however, I wish to indicate that to build up feelings of self-confidence the practice of suggesting confidence concepts to your mind is very effective. If your mind is obsessed by thoughts of insecurity and inadequacy it is, of course, due to the fact that such ideas have dominated your thinking over a long period of time. Another and more positive pattern of ideas must be given the mind, and that is accomplished by repetitive suggestion of confidence ideas. In the busy activities of daily existence thought disciplining is required if you are to re-educate the mind and make of it a power-producing plant. It is possible, even in the midst of your daily work, to drive confident thoughts into consciousness.

We build up the feeling of insecurity or security by how we

think. If in our thoughts we constantly fix attention upon sinister expectations of dire events that might happen, the result will be constantly to feel insecure. And what is even more serious is the tendency to create, by the power of thought, the very condition we fear.

Lack of self-confidence apparently is one of the great problems besetting people today. Everywhere you encounter people who are inwardly afraid, who shrink from life, who suffer from a deep sense of inadequacy and insecurity, who doubt their own powers. Deep within themselves they mistrust their ability to meet responsibilities or to grasp opportunities. Always they are beset by the vague and sinister fear that something is not going to be quite right. They do not believe that they have it in them to be what they want to be, and so they try to make themselves content with something less than that of which they are capable. Thousands upon thousands go crawling through life on their hands and knees, defeated and afraid. And in most cases such frustration of power is unnecessary.

The blows of life, the accumulation of difficulties, the multiplication of problems tend to sap energy and leave you spent and discouraged. In such a condition the true status of your power is often obscured, and a person yields to a discouragement that is not justified by the facts. It is vitally essential to re-appraise your personality assets. When done in an attitude of reasonableness, this evaluation will convince you that you are less defeated than you think you are.

The famous psychiatrist, Dr. Karl Menninger said, "Attitudes are more important than facts." That is worth repeating until its truth grips you. Any fact facing us, however difficult, even seemingly hopeless, is not so important as our attitude toward that fact. How you think about a fact may defeat you before you ever do anything about it. You may permit a fact to overwhelm you mentally before you start to deal with it actually. On the other hand, a confident and optimistic thought pattern can modify or overcome the fact altogether.

I know a man who is a tremendous asset to his organization, not because of any extraordinary ability, but because he invariably demonstrates a triumphant thought pattern. Perhaps his associates view a proposition pessimistically, so he employs what he calls "the vacuum-cleaner method." That is, by a series of questions he "sucks the dust" out of his associates' minds; he draws out their negative attitudes. Then quietly he suggests positive ideas concerning the proposition until a new set of attitudes gives them a new concept of the facts.

They often comment upon how different facts appear when this man "goes to work on them." It's the confidence attitude that makes the difference, nor does this rule out objectivity in an appraisal of facts. The inferiority complex victim sees all facts through discolored attitudes. The secret of correction is simply to gain a normal view, and that is always slanted on the positive side.

So if you feel that you are defeated and have lost confidence in your ability to win, sit down, take a piece of paper and make a list, not of the factors that are against you, but of those that are for you. If you or I or anybody think constantly of the forces that seem to be against us, we will build them up into a power far beyond that which is justified. They will assume a formidable strength which they do not actually possess. But if, on the contrary, you mentally visualize and affirm and reaffirm your assets and keep your thoughts on them, emphasizing them to the fullest extent, you will rise out of any difficulty regardless of what it may be. Your inner powers will reassert themselves and, with the help of God, lift you from defeat to victory.

One of the most powerful concepts, one which is a sure cure for lack of confidence, is the thought that God is actually with you and helping you. This is one of the simplest teachings in religion, namely, that Almighty God will be your companion, will stand by you, help you, and see you through. No other idea is so powerful in developing self-confidence as this simple belief when practiced. To practice it simply affirm "God is with me; God is helping me; God is guiding me." Spend several minutes each day visualizing His presence. Then practice believing that affirmation. Go about your business on the assumption that what you have affirmed and visualized is true. Affirm it, visualize it, believe it, and it will actualize itself. The release of power which this procedure stimulates will astonish you.

Feelings of confidence depend upon the type of thoughts that habitually occupy your mind. Think defeat and you are bound to feel defeated. But practice thinking confident thoughts, make it a dominating habit, and you will develop such a strong sense of capacity that regardless of what difficulties arise you will be able to overcome them. Feelings of confidence actually induce increased strength. Basil King once said, "Be bold, and mighty forces will come to your aid." Experience proves the truth of this. You will feel these mighty forces aiding you as your increasing faith reconditions your attitudes.

Emerson declared a tremendous truth, "They conquer who believe they can." And he added, "Do the thing you fear and the death of fear is certain." Practice confidence and faith and your fears and insecurities will soon have no power over you.

The secret is to fill your mind with thoughts of faith, confidence, and security. This will force out or expel all thoughts of doubt, all lack of confidence. To one man who for a long time had been haunted by insecurities and fears I suggested that he read through the Bible underlining in red pencil every statement it contains relative to courage and confidence. He also committed them to memory, in effect cramming his mind full of the healthiest, happiest, most powerful thoughts in the world. These dynamic thoughts changed him from cringing hopelessness to a man of compelling force. The change in him in a few weeks was remarkable. From almost complete defeat he became a confident and inspiring personality. He now radiates courage and magnetism.

He regained confidence in himself and his own powers by a simple process of thought conditioning.

To sum up — what can you do *now* to build up your self-confidence? Following are ten simple, workable rules for overcoming inadequacy attitudes and learning to practice faith. Thousands have used these rules, reporting successful results. Undertake this program and you, too, will build up confidence in your powers. You, too, will have a new feeling of power.

❧ **1.** Formulate and stamp indelibly on your mind a mental picture of yourself as succeeding. Hold this picture tenaciously. Never permit it to fade. Your mind will seek to develop this picture. Never think of yourself as failing; never doubt the reality of the mental image. That is most dangerous, for the mind always tries to complete what it pictures. So *always* picture "success" no matter how badly things seem to be going at the moment.

❧ **2.** Whenever a negative thought concerning your personal powers comes to mind, deliberately voice a positive thought to cancel it out.

❧ **3.** Do not build up obstacles in your imagination. Depreciate every so-called obstacle. Minimize them. Difficulties must be studied and efficiently dealt with to be eliminated, but they must be seen for only what they are. They must not be inflated by fear thoughts.

❧ **4.** Do not be awestruck by other people and try to copy them. Nobody can be you as efficiently as YOU can. Remember also that most people, despite their confident appearance and demeanor, are often as scared as you are and as doubtful of themselves.

❧ **5.** Ten times a day repeat these dynamic words, "If God be *for* us, who can be *against* us?" (Romans 8:31)
(Stop reading and repeat them NOW slowly and confidently.)

❧ **6.** Get a competent counselor to help you understand why you do what you do. Learn the origin of your inferiority and self-doubt feelings which often begin in childhood. Self-knowledge leads to a cure.

❧ **7.** Ten times each day practice the following affirmation, repeating it out loud if possible. "I can do all things through Christ which strengtheneth me." (Philippians 4:13) Repeat those words NOW. That magic statement is the most powerful antidote on earth to inferiority thoughts.

❧ **8.** Make a true estimate of your own ability, then raise it 10 per cent. Do not become egotistical, but develop a wholesome self-respect. Believe in your own God-released powers.

❧ **9.** Put yourself in God's hands. To do that simply state, "I am in God's hands." Then believe you are NOW receiving all the power you need. "Feel" it flowing into you. Affirm that "the kingdom of God is within you" (Luke 17:21) in the form of adequate power to meet life's demands.

❧ **10.** Remind yourself that God is with you and nothing can defeat you. Believe that you *now* RECEIVE power from Him.

❧ 2 ❧

A Peaceful Mind Generates Power

 The essence of the secret lies in a change of mental attitude. One must learn to live on a different thought basis, and even though thought change requires effort, it is much easier than to continue living as you are. The life of strain is difficult. The life of inner peace, being harmonious and without stress, is the easiest type of existence. The chief struggle then in gaining mental peace is the effort of revamping your thinking to the relaxed attitude of acceptance of God's gift of peace.

As a physician said, "Many of my patients have nothing wrong with them except their thoughts. So I have a favorite prescription that I write for some. But it is not a prescription that you can fill at a drugstore. The prescription I write is a verse from the Bible, 'Romans 12:2.' I do not write out that verse for my patients. I make them look it up and it reads: '. . . be ye transformed by the renewing of your mind . . .' To be happier and healthier they need a renewing of their minds, that is, a change in the pattern of their thoughts. When they 'take' this prescription, they actually achieve a mind full of peace. That helps to produce health and well-being."

A primary method for gaining a mind full of peace is to practice emptying the mind. This will be emphasized in another chapter, but I mention it here to underscore the importance of a frequent mental catharsis. I recommend a mind-emptying at least twice a day, more often if necessary. Definitely practice emptying your mind of fears, hates, insecurities, regrets, and guilt feelings. The mere fact that you consciously make this effort to empty your mind tends to give relief. Haven't you experienced a sense of release when you have been able to pour out to somebody whom you can trust worrisome matters that lay heavy upon the heart? As a pastor I have often observed how much it means to people to have someone to whom they can truly and in confidence tell everything troubling their minds.

Of course, emptying the mind is not enough. When the mind is emptied, something is bound to enter. The mind cannot long remain a vacuum. You cannot go around permanently with an empty mind. I admit that some people seem to accomplish that feat, but by and large it is necessary to refill the emptied mind or the old, unhappy thoughts which you have cast out will come sneaking in again.

To prevent that happening, immediately start filling your mind with creative and healthy thoughts. Then when the old fears, hates, and worries that have haunted you for so long try to edge back in, they will in effect find a sign on the door of your mind reading "occupied." They may struggle for admission, for having lived in your mind for a long time, they feel at home there. But the new and healthy thoughts which you have taken in will now be stronger and better fortified, and therefore able to repulse them. Presently the old thoughts will give up altogether and leave you alone. You will permanently enjoy a mind full of peace.

At intervals during the day practice thinking a carefully selected series of peaceful thoughts. Let mental pictures of the most peaceful scenes you have ever witnessed pass across your mind, as, for example, some beautiful valley filled with the hush of evening time, as the shadows lengthen and the sun sinks to rest. Or recall the silvery light of the moon falling upon rippling waters, or remember the sea washing gently upon soft shores of sand. Such peaceful thought images will work upon your mind as a healing medicine. So now and then during every day allow motion pictures of peace slowly to cross your mind.

Practice the technique of suggestive articulation, that is, repeat audibly some peaceful words. Words have profound suggestive power, and there is healing in the very saying of them. Utter a series of panicky words and your mind will immediately go into a mild state of nervousness. You will perhaps feel a sinking in the pit of your stomach that will affect your entire physical mechanism. If, on the contrary, you speak peaceful, quieting words, your mind will react in a peaceful manner. Use such a word as "tranquillity." Repeat that word slowly several times. *Tranquillity* is one of the most beautiful and melodic of all English words, and the mere saying of it tends to induce a tranquil state.

Another healing word is "serenity." Picturize serenity as you say it. Repeat it slowly and in the mood of which the word is a symbol. Words such as these have a healing potency when used in this manner.

It is also helpful to use lines from poetry or passages from the Scriptures. A man of my acquaintance who achieved a remarkable peace of mind has the habit of writing on cards unusual quotations expressing peacefulness. He carries one of the cards in his wallet at all times, referring to it frequently until each quotation is committed to memory. He says that each such idea dropped into the subconscious "lubricates" his mind with peace. A peaceful concept is indeed oil on troubled thoughts. One of the quotations which he used is from a sixteenth-century mystic, "Let nothing disturb you. Let nothing frighten you. Everything passes away except God. God alone is sufficient."

The words of the Bible have a particularly strong therapeutic value. Drop them into your mind, allowing them to "dissolve" in consciousness, and they will spread a healing balm over your entire mental structure. This is one of the simplest processes to perform and also one of the most effective in attaining peace of mind.

There are other practical ways by which you can develop serenity and quiet attitudes. One way is through your conversation. Depending upon the words we use and the tone in which we use them, we can talk ourselves into being nervous, high-strung, and upset. We can talk ourselves into either negative or positive results. By our speech we can also achieve quiet reactions. Talk peaceful to be peaceful.

In a group when the conversation takes a trend that is upsetting, try injecting peaceful ideas into the talk. Note how it counteracts the nervous tensions. Conversation filled with expressions of unhappy expectation, at breakfast, for example, often sets the tone of the day. Little wonder things turn out according to the unhappy specifications. Negative conversation adversely affects circumstances. Certainly talk of a tense and nervous nature enhances inner agitation.

On the contrary, start each day by affirming peaceful, contented, and happy attitudes and your days will tend to be pleasant and successful. Such attitudes are active and definite factors in creating satisfactory conditions. Watch your manner of speech then if you wish to develop a peaceful state of mind.

The words we speak have a direct and definite effect upon our thoughts. Thoughts create words, for words are the vehicles of ideas. But words also affect thoughts and help to condition if not to create attitudes. In fact, what often passes for thinking starts with talk. Therefore if the average conversation is scrutinized and disciplined to be sure that it contains peaceful expressions, the result will be peaceful ideas and ultimately, therefore, a peaceful mind.

Another effective technique in developing a peaceful mind is the daily practice of silence. Everyone should insist upon not less than a quarter of an hour of absolute quiet every twenty-four hours. Go alone into the quietest place available to you and sit or lie down for fifteen minutes and practice the art of silence. Do not talk to anyone. Do not write. Do not read. Think as little as possible. Throw your mind into neutral. Conceive of your mind as quiescent, inactive. This will not be easy at first because thoughts are stirring up your mind, but practice will increase your efficiency. Conceive of your mind as the surface of a body of water and see how nearly quiet you can make it, so that there is not a ripple. When you have attained a quiescent state, then begin to listen for the deeper sounds of harmony and beauty and of God that are to be found in the essence of silence.

In the circumstances of modern life, with its acceleration of pace, the practice of silence is admittedly not so simple as it was in the days of our forefathers. A vast number of noise-producing gadgets exist that they did not know, and our daily program is more hectic. Space has been annihilated in the modern world, and apparently we are also attempting to annihilate the factor of time. It is only rarely possible for an individual to walk in deep woods or sit by the sea or meditate on a mountaintop or on the deck of a vessel in the midst of the ocean. But when we do have such experiences, we can print on the mind the picture of the silent place and the feel of the moment and return to it in memory to live it over again just as truly as when we were actually in that scene. In fact, when you return to it in memory the mind tends to remove any unpleasant factors present in the actual situation. The memory visit is often an improvement over the actual for the mind tends to reproduce only the beauty in the remembered scene.

Fill your mind with all peaceful experiences possible, then make planned and deliberate excursions to them in memory. You must learn that the easiest way to an easy mind is to create an easy mind. This is done by practice, by the application of some such simple principles as outlined here. The mind quickly responds to teaching and discipline. You can make the mind give you back anything you want, but remember the mind can give back only what it was first given. Saturate your thoughts with peaceful experiences, peaceful words and ideas, and ultimately you will have a storehouse of peace-producing experiences to which you may turn for refreshment and renewal of your spirit. It will be a vast source of power.

There is a factor in the matter of inner peace which must be stated because of its importance. Frequently I find that people who are lacking in inner peace are victims of a self-punishment mechanism. At some time in their experience they have committed a sin and the sense of guilt haunts them. They have sincerely sought Divine forgiveness, and the good Lord will always forgive anyone who asks Him and who means it. However, there is a curious quirk within the human mind whereby sometimes an individual will not forgive himself.

He feels that he deserves punishment and therefore is constantly anticipating that punishment. As a result he lives in a constant apprehension that something is going to happen. In order to find peace under these circumstances he must increase the intensity of his activity. He feels that hard work will give him some release from his sense of guilt. A physician told me that in his practice a number of cases of nervous breakdown were traceable to a sense of guilt for which the patient had unconsciously attempted to compensate by hectic overwork. The patient attributed his breakdown not to the sense of guilt, but to his overworked condition. "But," said the physician, "these men need not have broken down from overwork if first the sense of guilt had been fully released." Peace of mind under such circumstances is available by yielding the guilt as well as the tension it produces to the healing therapy of Christ.

How To Have Constant Energy

 How we think we feel has a definite effect on how we actually feel physically. If your mind tells you that you are tired, the body mechanism, the nerves, and the muscles accept the fact. If your mind is intensely interested, you can keep on at an activity indefinitely. Religion functions through our thoughts, in fact, it is a system of thought discipline. By supplying attitudes of faith to the mind it can increase energy. It helps you to accomplish prodigious activity by suggesting that you have ample support and resources of power.

A friend in Connecticut, an energetic man, full of vitality and vigor, says that he goes to church regularly to "get his batteries recharged." His concept is sound. God *is* the source of all energy — energy in the universe, atomic energy, electrical energy, and spiritual energy; indeed every form of energy derives from the Creator. The Bible emphasizes this point when it says, "He giveth power to the faint; and to them that have no might he increaseth strength." (Isaiah 40:29)

In another statement the Bible describes the energizing and re-energizing process: ". . . in Him we live (that is, have vitality), and

14

move (have dynamic energy), and have our being (attain complete-ness)." (Acts 17:28)

Contact with God establishes within us a flow of the same type of energy that re-creates the world and that renews springtime every year. When in spiritual contact with God through our thought processes, the Divine energy flows through the personality, auto-matically renewing the original creative act. When contact with the Divine energy is broken, the personality gradually becomes depleted in body, mind, and spirit. An electric clock connected with an outlet does not run down and will continue indefinitely to keep accurate time. Unplug it, and the clock stops. It has lost con-tact with the power flowing through the universe. In general this process is operative in human experience though in a less mechanical manner.

Increasingly people are realizing that the maintenance of a sound spiritual life is important in enjoying energy and personality force.

The body is designed to produce all needed energy over an amazingly long period of time. If the individual takes reasonable care of his body from the standpoint of proper diet, exercise, sleep, no physical abuse, the body will produce and maintain astonishing energy and sustain itself in good health. If he gives similar attention to a well-balanced emotional life, energy will be conserved. But if he allows energy leaks caused by hereditary or self-imposed emotional reaction of a debilitating nature, he will be lacking in vital force. The natural state of the individual when body, mind, and spirit work harmoniously is that of a continuous replacement of necessary energy.

Every great personality I have ever known, and I have known many, who has demonstrated the capacity for prodigious work has been a person in tune with the Infinite. Every such person seems in harmony with nature and in contact with the Divine energy. They have not necessarily been pious people, but invariably they have been extraordinarily well organized from an emotional and psycho-logical point of view. It is fear, resentment, the projection of parental faults upon people when they are children, inner conflicts and obsessions that throw off balance the finely equated nature, thus causing undue expenditure of natural force.

The longer I live the more I am convinced that neither age nor circumstance needs to deprive us of energy and vitality. We are at last awakening to the close relationship between religion and health. We are beginning to comprehend a basic truth hitherto neglected, that our physical condition is determined very largely by our emotional condition, and our emotional life is profoundly regulated by our thought life.

All through its pages, the Bible talks about vitality and force and life. The supreme over-all word of the Bible is life, and life means vitality — to be filled with energy. Jesus stated the key expression, ". . . I am come that they might have life, and that they might have it more abundantly." (John 10:10) This does not rule out pain or suffering or difficulty, but the clear implication is that if a person practices the creative and re-creative principles of Christianity he can live with power and energy.

The practice of the above-mentioned principles will serve to bring a person into the proper tempo of living. Our energies are destroyed because of the high tempo, the abnormal pace at which we go. The conservation of energy depends upon getting your personality speed synchronized with the rate of God's movement. God is in you. If you are going at one rate and God at another, you are tearing yourself apart. "Though the mills of God grind slowly, yet they grind exceeding small." The mills of most of us grind very rapidly, and so they grind poorly. When we become attuned to God's rhythm we develop a normal tempo within ourselves and energy flows freely.

Everything is speeded up, and for that reason many people are tired. The solution is to get into the time synchronization of Almighty God. One way to do this is by going out some warm day and lying down on the earth. Get your ear close down to the ground and listen. You will hear all manner of sounds. You will

16

hear the sound of the wind in the trees and the murmur of insects, and you will discover presently that there is in all these sounds a well-regulated tempo. You cannot get that tempo by listening to traffic in the city streets, for it is lost in the confusion of sound. You can get it in church where you hear the word of God and the great hymns. Truth vibrates to God's tempo in a church. But you can also find it in a factory if you have a mind to.

A friend of mine, an industrialist in a large plant in Ohio, told me that the best workmen in his plant are those who get into harmony with the rhythm of the machine on which they are working. He declares that if a worker will work in harmony with the rhythm of his machine he will not be tired at the end of the day. He points out that the machine is an assembling of parts according to the law of God. When you love a machine and get to know it, you will be aware that it has a rhythm. It is one with the rhythm of the body, of the nerves, of the soul. It is in God's rhythm, and you can work with that machine and not get tired if you are in harmony with it. There is a rhythm of the stove, a rhythm of the typewriter, a rhythm of the office, a rhythm of an automobile, a rhythm of your job. So to avoid tiredness and to have energy, feel your way into the essential rhythm of Almighty God and all His works.

To accomplish this, relax physically. Then conceive of your mind as likewise relaxing. Follow this mentally by visualizing the soul as becoming quiescent, then pray as follows: "Dear God, You are the source of all energy. You are the source of the energy in the sun, in the atom, in all flesh, in the bloodstream, in the mind. I hereby draw energy from You as from an illimitable source." Then practice believing that you receive energy. Keep in tune with the Infinite.

Of course many people are tired simply because they are not interested in anything. Nothing ever moves them deeply. To some people it makes no difference what's going on or how things go. Their personal concerns are superior even to all crises in human

17

history. Nothing makes any real difference to them except their own little worries, their desires, and their hates. They wear themselves out stewing around about a lot of inconsequential things that amount to nothing. So they become tired. They even become sick. The surest way not to become tired is to lose yourself in something in which you have a profound conviction.

A famous statesman who made seven speeches in one day was still boundless in energy.

"Why are you not tired after making seven speeches?" I asked.

"Because," he said, "I believe absolutely in everything I said in those speeches. I am enthusiastic about my convictions."

That's the secret. He was on fire for something. He was pouring himself out, and you never lose energy and vitality in so doing. You only lose energy when life becomes dull in your mind. Your mind gets bored and therefore tired doing nothing. You don't have to be tired. Get interested in something. Get absolutely enthralled in something. Throw yourself into it with abandon. Get out of yourself. Be somebody. Do something. Don't sit around moaning about things, reading the papers, and saying, "Why don't they do something?" The man who is out doing something isn't tired. If you're not getting into good causes, no wonder you're tired. You're disintegrating. You're deteriorating. You're dying on the vine. The more you lose yourself in something bigger than yourself, the more energy you will have. You won't have time to think about yourself and get bogged down in your emotional difficulties.

To live with constant energy it is important to get your emotional faults corrected. You will never have full energy until you do.

The effect of guilt and fear feelings on energy is widely recognized by all authorities having to do with the problems of human nature. The quantity of vital force required to give the personality relief from either guilt or fear or a combination of each is so great that often only a fraction of energy remains for the discharge of the functions of living. Energy drainage occasioned by fear and

18

guilt is of such an amount as to leave little power to be applied to a person's job. The result is that he tires quickly. Not being able to meet the full requirements of his responsibility, he retreats into an apathetic, dull, listless condition and is indeed even ready to give up and fall back sleepily in a state of enervation.

A not infrequent case of diminishing energy is staleness. The pressure, monotony, and unceasing continuity of responsibilities dull the freshness of mind which a person must have to approach his work successfully. As an athlete goes stale so does the individual, whatever his occupation, tend to come upon dry and arid periods. During such a condition of mind the expenditure of greater energy is required to do with difficulty what one formerly did with comparative ease. As a result the vital powers are hard put to it to supply the force required, and the individual often loses his grip and power.

❊⟨ 4 ⟩❊

Try Prayer Power

Experts in physical health and well-being often utilize prayer in their therapy. Disability, tension, and kindred troubles may result from a lack of inner harmony. It is remarkable how prayer restores the harmonious functioning of body and soul. A friend of mine, a physiotherapist, told a nervous man to whom he was giving a massage, "God works through my fingers as I seek to relax your physical body, which is the temple of your soul. While I work on your outward being, I want you to pray for God's relaxation inwardly." It was a new idea to the patient, but he happened to be in a receptive mood and he tried passing some peace thoughts through his mind. He was amazed at the relaxing effect this had on him.

People are doing more praying today than formerly because they find that it adds to personal efficiency. Prayer helps them to tap forces and to utilize strength not otherwise available.

A famous psychologist says, "Prayer is the greatest power available to the individual in solving his personal problems. Its power astonishes me."

Prayer power is manifestation of energy. Just as there exist scientific techniques for the release of atomic energy, so are there scientific procedures for the release of spiritual energy through the mechanism of prayer. Exciting demonstrations of this energizing force are evident.

Prayer power seems able even to normalize the aging process, obviating or limiting infirmity and deterioration. You need not lose your basic energy or vital power or become weak and listless merely as a result of accumulating years. It is not necessary to allow your spirit to sag or grow stale or dull. Prayer can freshen you up every evening and send you out renewed each morning. You can receive guidance in problems if prayer is allowed to permeate your subconscious, the seat of the forces which determines whether you take right or wrong actions. Prayer has the power to keep your reactions correct and sound. Prayer driven deeply into your subconscious can remake you. It releases and keeps power flowing freely.

If you have not experienced this power, perhaps you need to learn new techniques of prayer. It is well to study prayer from an efficiency point of view. Usually the emphasis is entirely religious though no cleavage exists between the two concepts. Scientific spiritual practice rules out stereotyped procedure even as it does in general science. If you have been praying in a certain manner, even if it has brought you blessings, which it doubtless has, perhaps you can pray even more profitably by varying the pattern and by experimenting with fresh prayer formulas. Get new insights; practice new skills to attain greatest results.

It is important to realize that you are dealing with the most tremendous power in the world when you pray. You would not use an old-fashioned kerosene lamp for illumination. You want the most up-to-date lighting devices. New and fresh spiritual techniques are being constantly discovered by men and women of spiritual genius. It is advisable to experiment with prayer power according to such methods as prove sound and effective. If this sounds new and strangely scientific, bear in mind that the secret of prayer is to find the process that will most effectively open your mind humbly to God. Any method through which you can stimulate the power of God to flow into your mind is legitimate and usable.

A man opened a small business in New York City a number of years ago, his first establishment being, as he characterized it, "a little hole in the wall." He had one employee. In a few years they moved into a larger room and then into extensive quarters. It became a very successful operation.

This man's method of business as he described it was "to fill the little hole in the wall with optimistic prayers and thoughts." He declared that hard work, positive thinking, fair dealing, right treatment of people, and the proper kind of praying always get results. This man, who has a creative and unique mind, worked out his own simple formula for solving his problems and overcoming his difficulties through prayer power. It is a curious formula but I have practiced it and personally know that it works. I have suggested it to many people who also found real value in its use. It is recommended to you. The formula is:

(1) PRAYERIZE   (2) PICTURIZE   (3) ACTUALIZE.

By "prayerize" my friend meant a daily system of creative prayer. When a problem arose he talked it over with God very simply and directly in prayer. Moreover, he did not talk with God as to some vast and far-off shadowy being but conceived of God as being with him in his office, in his home, on the street, in his automobile, always near by as a partner, as a close associate. He took seriously the Biblical injunction to "pray without ceasing." He interpreted it as meaning that he should go about every day discussing with God in a natural, normal manner the questions that had to be decided and dealt with. The Presence came finally to dominate his conscious and ultimately his unconscious thinking. He "prayerized" his daily life. He prayed as he walked or drove his car or performed other everyday activities. He filled his daily life full of prayer — that is, he lived by prayer. He did not often kneel to offer his prayers but would, for example, say to God as to a close associate, "What will I do about this, Lord?" or "Give me a fresh insight on this, Lord." He prayerized his mind and so prayerized his activities.

The second point in his formula of creative prayer is to "picturize." The basic factor in physics is force. The basic factor in psychology is the realizable wish. The man who assumes success tends already to have success. People who assume failure tend to have failure. When either failure or success is picturized it strongly tends to actualize in terms equivalent to the mental image pictured.

To assure something worth while happening, first pray about it and test it according to God's will; then print a picture of it on your mind as happening, holding the picture firmly in consciousness. Continue to surrender the picture to God's will — that is to say, put the matter in God's hands — and follow God's guidance. Work hard and intelligently, thus doing your part to achieve success in the matter. Practice believing and continue to hold the picturization firmly in your thoughts. Do this and you will be astonished at the strange ways in which the picturization comes to pass. In this manner the picture "actualizes." That which you have "prayerized" and "picturized" "actualizes" according to the pattern of your basic realizable wish when conditioned by invoking God's power upon it, and if, moreover, you give fully of yourself to its realization.

I have personally practiced this three-point prayer method and find great power in it. It has been suggested to others who have likewise reported that it released creative power into their experience.

Personally, I believe that prayer is a sending out of vibrations from one person to another and to God. All of the universe is in vibration. There are vibrations in the molecules of a table. The air is filled with vibrations. The reaction between human beings is also in vibration. When you send out a prayer for another person, you employ the force inherent in a spiritual universe. You transport from yourself to the other person a sense of love, helpfulness, support — a sympathetic, powerful understanding — and in this process you awaken vibrations in the universe through which God brings to pass the good objectives prayed for. Experiment with this principle and you will know its amazing results.

For example, I have a habit, which I often use, of praying for people as I pass them. I remember being on a train traveling through West Virginia when I had a curious thought. I saw a man standing on a station platform, then the train moved on and he passed from sight. It occurred to me that I was seeing him for the first and last time. His life and mine touched lightly for just a fraction of an instant. He went his way and I went mine. I wondered how his life would turn out.

One of the important functions of prayer is as a stimulus to creative ideas. Within the mind are all of the resources needed for successful living. Ideas are present in consciousness which, when released and given scope together with proper implementation, can lead to the successful operation of any project or undertaking. When the New Testament says, "The kingdom of God is within you," (Luke 17:21) it is informing us that God our Creator has laid up within our minds and personalities all the potential powers and ability we need for constructive living. It remains for us to tap and develop these powers.

Alert people everywhere are finding that by trying prayer power they feel better, work better, do better, sleep better, are better.

Following are ten rules for getting effective results from prayer:

❧**1.** Set aside a few minutes every day. Do not say anything. Simply practice thinking about God. This will make your mind spiritually receptive.

❧**2.** Then pray orally, using simple, natural words. Tell God anything that is on your mind. Do not think you must use stereotyped pious phrases. Talk to God in your own language. He understands it.

❧**3.** Pray as you go about the business of the day, on the subway or bus or at your desk. Utilize minute prayers by closing your eyes to shut out the world and concentrating briefly on God's presence. The more you do this every day the nearer you will feel God's presence.

❧ **4.** Do not always ask when you pray, but instead affirm that God's blessings are being given, and spend most of your prayers giving thanks.

❧ **5.** Pray with the belief that sincere prayers can reach out and surround your loved ones with God's love and protection.

❧ **6.** Never use a negative thought in prayer. Only positive thoughts get results.

❧ **7.** Always express willingness to accept God's will. Ask for what you want, but be willing to take what God gives you. It may be better than what you ask for.

❧ **8.** Practice the attitude of putting everything in God's hands. Ask for the ability to do your best and to leave the results confidently to God.

❧ **9.** Pray for people you do not like or who have mistreated you. Resentment is blockade number one of spiritual power.

❧ **10.** Make a list of people for whom to pray. The more you pray for other people, especially those not connected with you, the more prayer results will come back to you.

✢{ 5 }✢

How To Create Your Own Happiness

Who decides whether you shall be happy or unhappy? The answer — you do!

I recall that Abraham Lincoln said that people were just about as happy as they made up their minds to be. You can be unhappy if you want to be. It is the easiest thing in the world to accomplish. Just choose unhappiness. Go around telling yourself that things aren't going well, that nothing is satisfactory, and you can be quite sure of being unhappy. But say to yourself, "Things are going nicely. Life is good. I choose happiness," and you can be quite certain of having your choice.

Children are more expert in happiness than adults. The adult who can carry the spirit of a child into middle and old age is a genius, for he will preserve the truly happy spirit with which God endowed the young. The subtlety of Jesus Christ is remarkable, for He tells us that the way to live in this world is to have the childlike heart and mind. In other words, never get old or dull or jaded in spirit. Don't become super-sophisticated.

A group of boys and girls were asked to list the things that made them happiest. Their answers were rather touching. Here is the boys' list: "A swallow flying; looking into deep, clear water; water being cut at the bow of a boat; a fast train rushing; a builder's crane lifting something heavy; my dog's eyes."

And here is what the girls said made them happy: "Street lights on the river; red roofs in the trees; smoke rising from a chimney; red velvet; the moon in the clouds." There is something in the beautiful essence of the universe that is expressed, though only half-articulated, by these things. To become a happy person have a clean soul, eyes that see romance in the commonplace, a child's heart, and spiritual simplicity.

Many of us manufacture our own unhappiness. Of course not all unhappiness is self-created, for social conditions are responsible for not a few of our woes. Yet it is a fact that to a large extent by our thoughts and attitudes we distill out of the ingredients of life either happiness or unhappiness for ourselves.

"Four people out of five are not so happy as they can be," declares an eminent authority, and he adds, "Unhappiness is the most common state of mind." Whether human happiness strikes as low a level as this, I would hesitate to say, but I do find more people living unhappy lives than I would care to compute. Since a fundamental desire of every human being is for that state of existence called happiness, something should be done about it. Happiness is achievable and the process for obtaining it is not complicated. Anyone who desires it, who wills it, and who learns and applies the right formula may become a happy person.

Rather than to emphasize the manner in which people manufacture their own unhappiness, let us proceed to the formula for putting an end to this misery-producing process. Suffice it to say that we manufacture our unhappiness by thinking unhappy thoughts, by the attitudes which we habitually take, such as the negative feeling that everything is going to turn out badly, or that other people are getting what they do not deserve and we are failing to get what we do deserve.

Our unhappiness is further distilled by saturating the consciousness with feelings of resentment, ill will, and hate. The unhappiness-producing process always makes important use of the ingredients of fear and worry. Each of these matters is dealt with elsewhere in this book. We merely want to make the point at the present time and stress it forcefully that a very large proportion of the unhappiness of the average individual is self-manufactured. How, then, may we proceed to produce not unhappiness but happiness?

The happiness habit is developed by simply practicing happy thinking. Make a mental list of happy thoughts and pass them through your mind several times every day. If an unhappiness thought should enter your mind, immediately stop, consciously eject it, and substitute a happiness thought. Every morning before arising, lie relaxed in bed and deliberately drop happy thoughts into your conscious mind. Let a series of pictures pass across your mind of each happy experience you expect to have during the day. Savor their joy. Such thoughts will help cause events to turn out that way. Do not affirm that things will not go well that day. By merely saying that, you can actually help to make it so. You will draw to yourself every factor, large and small, that will contribute to unhappy conditions. As a result, you will find yourself asking, "Why does everything go badly for me? What is the matter with everything?"

The reason can be directly traced to the manner in which you began the day in your thoughts.

Tomorrow try this plan instead. When you arise, say out loud three times this one sentence, "This is the day which the Lord hath made; we will rejoice and be glad in it." (Psalm 118:24) Only personalize it and say, "I will rejoice and be glad in it." Repeat it in a strong, clear voice and with positive tone and emphasis. The statement, of course, is from the Bible and it is a good cure for unhappiness. If you repeat that one sentence three times before breakfast and meditate on the meaning of the words you will change the character of the day by starting off with a happiness psychology.

While dressing or shaving or getting breakfast, say aloud a few such remarks as the following, "I believe this is going to be a wonderful day. I believe I can successfully handle all problems that will arise today. I feel good physically, mentally, emotionally. It is wonderful to be alive. I am grateful for all that I have had, for all that I now have, and for all that I shall have. Things aren't going to fall apart. God is here and He is with me and He will see me through. I thank God for every good thing."

But it is not sufficient to apply to the mind even such an important affirmation therapy as I have just suggested unless throughout the day you also base your actions and attitudes upon fundamental principles of happy living.

One of the most simple and basic of such principles is that of human love and good will. It is amazing what happiness a sincere expression of compassion and tenderness will induce.

Of course in order to give power to these principles of happiness and make them work it is necessary to support them with a dynamic quality of mind. You are not likely to secure effective results even with spiritual principles without spiritual power. When one experiences a dynamic spiritual change inwardly, success with happiness-producing ideas becomes extraordinarily easy. If you begin to use spiritual principles, however awkwardly, you will gradually experience spiritual power inwardly. I can assure you that this will give you the greatest surge of happiness you have ever known. It will stay with you, too, as long as you live a God-centered life.

In my travels about the country I have been encountering an increasing number of genuinely happy individuals. These are persons who have been practicing the techniques described in this book and which I have presented in other volumes and in other writings and talks and which other writers and speakers have likewise been giving to receptive people. It is astonishing how people can become inoculated with happiness through an inner experience of spiritual change. People of all types everywhere are having this experience today. In fact, it has become one of the most popular phenomena of our times, and if it continues to develop and expand, the person who has not had a spiritual experience will soon be considered old-fashioned and behind the times. Nowadays it is smart to be spiritually alive. It is old-fogyism to be ignorant of that happiness-producing transformation which people everywhere are enjoying at this time.

As you read this book believe what you read, because it is true; then start working on the practical suggestions the book contains and you, too, will have the spiritual experience that produces this quality of happiness. I know this is so, because many of those to whom I have referred and shall refer in later chapters got their vital new life in the same way. Then, having been changed inwardly, you will begin to create out of yourself not unhappiness, but a happiness of such quality and character that you will wonder if you are living in the same world. As a matter of fact it won't be the same world because you are not the same, and what you are determines the world in which you live, so as you change, your world changes also.

❊⟨ 6 ⟩❊

Stop Fuming And Fretting

 Many people make life unnecessarily difficult for themselves by dissipating power and energy through fuming and fretting.

Do you ever "fume" and "fret"? Here is a picture of yourself if you do. The word "fume" means to boil up, to blow off, to emit vapor, to be agitated, to be distraught, to seethe. The word "fret" is equally descriptive. It is reminiscent of a sick child in the night, a petulant half-cry, half-whine. It ceases, only to begin again. It has an irritating, annoying, penetrating quality. To fret is a childish term, but it describes the emotional reaction of many adults.

The Bible advises us to "Fret not thyself . . ." (Psalm 37:1) This is sound advice for the people of our time. We need to stop fuming and fretting and get peaceful if we are to have power to live effectively. And how do we go about doing so?

A first step is to reduce your pace or at least the tempo of your pace. We do not realize how accelerated the rate of our lives has become, or the speed at which we are driving ourselves. Many people are destroying their physical bodies by this pace, but what is even more tragic, they are tearing their minds and souls to shreds as well. It is possible for a person to live a quiet existence physically and yet maintain a high tempo emotionally. Even an invalid can live at too high a pace from that standpoint. The character of our thoughts determines pace. When the mind goes rushing on pell-mell from one feverish attitude to another it becomes feverish and the result is a state bordering on petulance. The pace of modern life must be reduced if we are not to suffer profoundly from its debilitating over-stimulation and super-excitement. This over-stimulation produces toxic poisons in the body and creates emotional illness. It produces fatigue and a sense of frustration so that we fume and fret about everything from our personal troubles to the state of the nation and the world. If the effect of this emotional disquiet is so pronounced physically, what must its effect be on that deep inner essence of the personality known as the soul?

It is impossible to have peace of soul if the pace is so feverishly accelerated. God won't go that fast. He will not endeavor to keep up with you. He says in effect, "Go ahead if you must with this foolish pace and when you are worn out I will offer my healing. But I can make your life so rich if you will slow down now and live and move and have your being in me." God moves imperturbably, slowly, and with perfect organization. The only wise rate at which to live is God's rate. God gets things done and they are done right and He does them without hurry. He neither fumes nor frets. He is peaceful and therefore efficient. This same peace is offered to us — "Peace I leave with you, my peace I give unto you . . ." (John 14:27)

Peace is still to be found in America in our woods and great plains, in our valleys, in our mountain majesties, and where the ocean foams on soft shores of sand. We should avail ourselves of its healing. Remember the words of Jesus, "Come ye yourselves apart into a desert place, and rest awhile." (Mark 6:31) Even as I write these words and give you this good advice, I recall instances where it has been necessary to remind myself to practice the same truth, which emphasizes that we must everlastingly discipline ourselves to quietness if we expect its benefits in our lives.

Have you ever considered the importance of having the peace of God in your muscles, in your joints? Perhaps your joints will not pain so much when they have the peace of God in them. Your muscles will work with correlation when the peace of God who created them governs their action. Speak to your muscles every day and to your joints and to your nerves, saying, "Fret not thyself." (Psalm 37:1) Relax on a couch or bed, think of each important muscle from head to feet, and say to each, "The peace of God is touching you." Then practice "feeling" that peace throughout your entire body. In due course your muscles and joints will take heed.

Slow down, for whatever you really want will be there when you get there if you work toward it without stress, without pressing. If, proceeding under God's guidance and in His smooth and unhurried tempo, it is not there, then it was not supposed to be there. If you miss it, perhaps you should have missed it. So definitely seek to develop a normal, natural, God-ordered pace. Practice and preserve mental quiet. Learn the art of letting go all nervous excitement. To do this, stop at intervals and affirm, "I now relinquish nervous excitement — it is flowing from me. I am at peace." Do not fume. Do not fret. Practice being peaceful.

To attain this efficient state of living, I recommend the practice of thinking peaceful thoughts. Every day we perform a series of acts designed to care for the body properly. We bathe, brush the teeth, take exercise. In similar fashion we should give time and planned effort to keeping the mind in a healthy state. One way to do this is to sit quietly and pass a series of peaceful thoughts through the mind. For example, pass through the thoughts the memory of a lofty mountain, a misty valley, a sun-speckled trout stream, silver moonlight on water.

At least once in every twenty-four hours, preferably in the busiest part of the day, deliberately stop whatever you are doing for ten or fifteen minutes and practice serenity.

There are times when it is essential resolutely to check our headlong pace, and it must be emphasized that the only way to stop is to stop.

In attaining emotional control the daily practice of healing techniques is of first importance. Emotional control cannot be gained in any magical or easy way. You cannot develop it by merely reading a book, although that is often helpful. The only sure method is by working at it regularly, persistently, scientifically, and by developing creative faith.

I suggest that you begin with such a primary procedure as simply the practice of keeping physically still. Don't pace the floor. Don't wring your hands. Don't pound or shout or argue or walk up and down. Don't let yourself get worked up into a dither. In excitement one's physical movements become accentuated. Therefore begin at the simplest place, that is by ceasing physical movement. Stand still, sit down, lie down. Certainly keep the voice down to a low pitch.

In developing a calm control it is necessary to think calmness, for the body responds sensitively to the type of thoughts that pass through the mind. It is also true that the mind can be quieted by first making the body quiet. That is to say, a physical attitude can induce desired mental attitudes.

It is, moreover, a good procedure to practice being phlegmatic or apathetic, even indifferent. To a certain extent even practice being sluggish. People thus constituted are less likely to emotional breaks. Highly organized individuals may do well to cultivate these reactions to a degree at least.

Naturally one does not want to lose the keen, sensitive responsiveness characteristic of the highly organized individual. But the practice of being phlegmatic tends to bring such a keyed-up personality to a balanced emotional position.

Following is a technique consisting of six points which I have personally found of great helpfulness in reducing the tendency to fume and fret. I have suggested its use to countless people who practice it and find it of great value:

❧**1.** Sit relaxed in a chair. Completely yield yourself to the chair. Starting with your toes and proceeding to the top of your head, conceive every portion of the body as relaxing. Affirm relaxation by saying, "My toes are relaxed — my fingers — my facial muscles."

❧**2.** Think of your mind as the surface of a lake in a storm, tossed by waves and in tumult. But now the waves subside, and the surface of the lake is placid and unruffled.

❧**3.** Spend two or three minutes thinking of the most beautiful and peaceful scenes you have ever beheld, as, for example, a mountain at sunset, or a deep valley filled with the hush of early morning, or a woods at noonday, or moonlight upon rippling waters. In memory relive these scenes.

❧**4.** Repeat slowly, quietly, bringing out the melody in each, a series of words which express quietness and peace, as, for example, (a) tranquillity (say it very deliberately and in a tranquil manner); (b) serenity, (c) quietness. Think of other such words and repeat them.

❧**5.** Make a mental list of times in your life when you have been conscious of God's watchful care and recall how, when you were worried and anxious, He brought things out right and took care of you. Then recite aloud this line from an old hymn, "So long Thy power hath kept me, sure it STILL will lead me on."

❧**6.** Repeat the following, which has an amazing power to relax and quiet the mind: "Thou wilt keep him in perfect peace, whose mind is stayed on thee." (Isaiah 26:3) Repeat this several times during the day, whenever you have a fraction of a moment. Repeat it aloud if possible, so that by the end of the day you will have said it many times. Conceive of these words as active, vital substances permeating your mind, sending into every area of your

35

thinking a healing balm. This is the best-known medicine for taking tension from the mind.

As you work with the techniques suggested in this chapter, the tendency to fume and fret will gradually be modified. In direct proportion to your progress the power heretofore drawn off by this unhappy habit will be felt in your increased abililty to meet life's responsibilities.

❊(7)❊

Expect The Best And Get It

 Learn to expect, not to doubt. In so doing you bring everything into the realm of possibility.

This does not mean that by believing you are necessarily going to get everything you want or think you want. Perhaps that would not be good for you. When you put your trust in God, He guides your mind so that you do not want things that are not good for you or that are inharmonious with God's will. But it does definitely mean that when you learn to believe, then that which has seemingly been impossible moves into the area of the possible. Every great thing at last becomes for you a possibility.

William James, the famous psychologist, said, "Our belief at the beginning of a doubtful undertaking is the one thing (now get that — *is the one thing*) that insures the successful outcome of your venture." To learn to believe is of primary importance. It is the basic factor of succeeding in any undertaking. When you expect the best, you release a magnetic force in your mind which by a law of attraction tends to bring the best to you. But if you expect the worst, you release from your mind the power of repulsion which tends to force the best from you. It is amazing how a sustained expectation of the best sets in motion forces which cause the best to materialize.

Perhaps you have not been doing so well in the game of life. Perhaps you stand up to bat and cannot make a hit. You strike out time and again and your batting average is lamentably low. Let me give you a suggestion. I guarantee that it will work. The basis for my assurance is the fact that thousands of people have been trying it with very great results. Things will be very different for you if you give this method a real trial.

Start reading the New Testament and notice the number of times it refers to faith. Select a dozen of the strongest statements about faith, the ones that you like the best. Then memorize each one. Let these faith concepts drop into your conscious mind. Say them over and over again, especially just before going to sleep at night. By a process of spiritual osmosis they will sink from your conscious into your subconscious mind and in time will modify and reslant your basic thought pattern. This process will change you into a believer, into an expecter, and when you become such, you will in due course become an achiever. You will have new power to get what God and you decide you really want from life.

The most powerful force in human nature is the spiritual-power technique taught in the Bible. Very astutely the Bible emphasizes the method by which a person can make something of himself. Faith, belief, positive thinking, faith in God, faith in other people, faith in yourself, faith in life. This is the essence of the technique that it teaches. "If thou canst believe," it says, "all things are possible to him that believeth." (Mark 9:23) "If ye have faith . . . nothing shall be impossible unto you." (Matthew 17:20) "According to your faith be it unto you." (Matthew 9:29) Believe — believe — so it drives home the truth that faith moves mountains.

Some skeptical person who has never learned this powerful law of the effect of right thinking may doubt my assertions regarding the amazing results which happen when this technique is employed.

Things become better when you expect the best instead of the worst, for the reason that being freed from self-doubt, you can put your whole self into your endeavor, and nothing can stand in the way of the man who focuses his entire self on a problem. When you approach a difficulty as a personal unity, the difficulty, which itself is a demonstration of disunity, tends to deteriorate.

When the entire concentration of all your force — physical, emotional, and spiritual — is brought to bear, the consolidation of these powers properly employed is quite irresistible.

Expecting the best means that you put your whole heart (i.e., the central essence of your personality) into what you want to accomplish. People are defeated in life not because of lack of ability, but for lack of wholeheartedness. They do not wholeheartedly expect to succeed. Their heart isn't in it, which is to say they themselves are not fully given. Results do not yield themselves to the person who refuses to give himself to the desired results.

A major key to success in this life, attaining that which you deeply desire, is to be completely released and throw all there is of yourself into your job or any project in which you are engaged. In other words, whatever you are doing, give it all you've got. Give every bit of yourself. Hold nothing back. Life cannot deny itself to the person who gives life his all. But most people, unfortunately, don't do that. In fact, very few people do, and this is a tragic cause of failure, or, if not failure, it is the reason we only half attain.

Don't be a "holdout." Go all out. Do this, and life will not hold out on you.

A famous trapeze artist was instructing his students how to perform on the high trapeze bar. Finally, having given full explanations and instructions in this skill, he told them to demonstrate their ability.

One student, looking up at the insecure perch upon which he must perform, was suddenly filled with fear. He froze completely. He had a terrifying vision of himself falling to the ground. He couldn't move a muscle, so deep was his fright. "I can't do it! I can't do it!" he gasped.

The instructor put his arm around the boy's shoulder and said, "Son, you can do it, and I will tell you how." Then he made a statement which is of inestimable importance. It is one of the wisest remarks I have ever heard. He said, "Throw your heart over the bar and your body will follow."

Copy that one sentence. Write it on a card and put it in your pocket. Place it under the glass on your desk top. Tack it up on your wall. Stick it in your shaving mirror. Better still, write it on your mind, you who really want to do something with life. It's packed with power, that sentence. "Throw your heart over the bar and your body will follow."

Heart is the symbol of creative activity. Fire the heart with where you want to go and what you want to be. Get it so deeply fixed in your unconscious that you will not take no for an answer, then your entire personality will follow where your heart leads. "Throw your heart over the bar" means to throw your faith over your difficulty, throw your affirmation over every barrier, throw your visualization over your obstacles. In other words, throw the spiritual essence of you over the bar and your material self will follow in the victory groove thus pioneered by your faith-inspired mind. Expect the best, not the worst, and you will attain your heart's desire. It is what is in the heart of you, either good or bad, strong or weak, that finally comes to you. Emerson said, "Beware of what you want for you will get it."

The formula is to know what you want, test it to see if it is a right thing, change yourself in such a manner that it will naturally come to you, and always have faith. With the creative force of belief you stimulate that particular gathering together of circumstances which brings your cherished wish to pass.

Students of modern dynamic thought are realizing more and more the practical value of the ideas and teachings of Jesus, especially such truths as the dictum, "According to your faith, be it unto you." (Matthew 9:29) According to your faith in yourself, according to your faith in your job, according to your faith in God, this far will you get and no further. If you believe in your job and in yourself and in the opportunities of your country, and if you believe in God and will work hard and study and put yourself into it — in other words, if you "throw your heart over the bar," you can swing up to any high place to which you want to take your life and your service and your achievement. Whenever you have a bar, that is to say a barrier, in front of you, stop, close your eyes, visualize everything that is above the bar and nothing that is below it, then imaginatively throw "your heart" over that bar and see yourself as being given lifting power to rise above it. Believe that you are experiencing this upthrust of force. You will be amazed at the lifting force you will receive. If in the depth of your mind you visualize the best and employ the powers of faith and energy, you will get the best.

Naturally in this process of achieving the best it is important to know where you want to go in life. You can reach your goal, your best dreams can come true, you can get where you want to go only if you know what your goal is. Your expectation must have a clearly defined objective. Lots of people get nowhere simply because they do not know where they want to go. They have no clear-cut, precisely defined purpose. You cannot expect the best if you think aimlessly.

It is indeed a fact that the person who thinks with positive self-reliance and optimism does magnetize his condition and releases power to attain his goal. So expect the best at all times. Never think of the worst. Drop it out of your thought, relegate it. Let there be no thought in your mind that the worst will happen. Avoid entertaining the concept of the worst, for whatever you take into your mind can grow there. Therefore take the best into your mind and only that. Nurture it, concentrate on it, emphasize it, visualize it, prayerize it, surround it with faith. Make it your obsession. Expect the best, and spiritually creative mind power aided by God power will produce the best.

It may be that as you read this book you are down to what you think is the worst and you may remark that no amount of thinking will affect your situation. The answer to that objection is that it simply isn't so. Even if you may be down to the worst, the best is potentially within you. You have only to find it, release it, and rise up with it. This requires courage and character, to be sure, but the main requirement is faith. Cultivate faith and you will have the necessary courage and character.

It is a well-defined and authentic principle that what the mind profoundly expects it tends to receive. Perhaps this is true because what you really expect is what you actually want. Unless you really want something sufficiently to create an atmosphere of positive factors by your dynamic desire, it is likely to elude you. "If with all your heart" — that is the secret. "If with all your heart," that is to say, if with the full complement of your personality, you reach out creatively toward your heart's desire, your reach will not be in vain.

Let me give you four words as a formulation of a great law — *faith power works wonders*. Those four words are packed with dynamic and creative force. Hold them in your conscious mind. Let them sink into the unconscious and they can help you to overcome any difficulty. Hold them in your thoughts, say them over and over again. Say them until your mind accepts them, until you believe them — *faith power works wonders*.

I have no doubt about the effectiveness of this concept, for I have seen it work so often that my enthusiasm for faith power is absolutely boundless.

You can overcome any obstacle. You can achieve the most tremendous things by faith power. And how do you develop faith power? The answer is: to saturate your mind with the great words of the Bible. If you will spend one hour a day reading the Bible and committing its great passages to memory, thus allowing them to recondition your personality, the change in you and in your experience will be little short of miraculous.

Just one section of the Bible will accomplish this for you. The eleventh chapter of Mark is enough. You will find the secret in the following words, and this is one of the greatest formulas the Book contains: "Have faith in God (that's positive, isn't it?) for verily I say unto you, that whosoever shall say unto *this* mountain (that's specific) be thou removed (that is, stand aside) and be thou cast into the sea (that means out of sight — anything you throw into the sea is gone for good. The *Titanic* lies at the bottom of the sea. And the sea bottom is lined with ships. Cast your opposition called a "mountain" into the sea) and shall not doubt in his heart (Why does this statement use the word heart? Because it means you are not to doubt in your subconscious, in the inner essence of you. It isn't so superficial as a doubt in the conscious mind. That is a normal, intelligent questioning. It's a deep fundamental doubt that is to be avoided) but shall believe that those things which he saith shall come to pass, he shall have whatsoever he saith." (Mark 11: 22-23)

This is not some theory that I have thought up. It is taught by the most reliable book known to man. Generation after generation, no matter what develops in the way of knowledge and science, the Bible is read by more people than any other book. Humanity rightly has more confidence in it than any other document ever written, and the Bible tells us that faith power works wonders.

The reason, however, that great things do not happen to some people is that they are not specific in their application of faith power. We are told, "Ye shall say to *this* mountain." That is to say, do not address your efforts to the entire mountain range of all your difficulties, but attack one thing that may be defeating you at the moment. Be specific. Take them one by one.

If there is something you want, how do you go about getting it? In the first place, ask yourself, "Should I want it?" Test that question very honestly in prayer to be sure you should want it and whether you should have it. If you can answer that question in the affirmative, then ask God for it and don't be backward in asking Him. And if God, having more insight, believes that you shouldn't

43

have it, you needn't worry — He won't give it to you. But if it is a right thing, ask Him for it, and when you ask, do not doubt in your heart. Be specific.

Be specific. Ask God for any right thing, but as a little child, don't doubt. Doubt closes the power flow. Faith opens it. The power of faith is so tremendous that there is nothing that Almighty God cannot do for us, with us, or through us if we let Him channel His power through our minds.

So roll those words around on your tongue. Say them over and over again until they lodge deeply in your mind, until they get down into your heart, until they take possession of the essence of you: ". . . whosoever shall say unto this mountain, be thou removed, and be thou cast into the sea, and shall not doubt in his heart, but shall believe that those things which he saith shall come to pass, he shall have whatsoever he saith." (Mark 11:23)

Every day as you confront the problems of life, I suggest that you affirm as follows: "I believe God gives me power to attain what I really want."

Never mention the worst. Never think of it. Drop it out of your consciousness. At least ten times every day affirm, "I expect the best and with God's help will attain the best."

In so doing your thoughts will turn toward the best and become conditioned to its realization. This practice will bring all of your powers to focus upon the attainment of the best. It will bring the best to you.

❧ 8 ❧

I Don't Believe In Defeat

 If you are thinking thoughts of defeat, I urge you to rid yourself of such thoughts, for as you think defeat you tend to get it. Adopt the "I don't believe in defeat" attitude.

I shall explain the techniques and formulas by which you, too, can overcome defeats which at the present moment may seem inevitable.

The first thing to do about an obstacle is simply to stand up to it and not complain about it or whine under it but forthrightly attack it. Don't go crawling through life on your hands and knees half-defeated. Stand up to your obstacles and do something about them. You will find that they haven't half the strength you think they have.

Faith supplies staying power. It contains dynamics to keep one going when the going is hard. Anybody can keep going when the going is good, but some extra ingredient is needed to enable you to keep fighting when it seems that everything is against you. It is a great secret, that of never being "defeated by the discouraging vicissitudes of the game."

You may counter, "But you don't know my circumstances. I am

in a different situation than anybody else and I am as far down as a human being can get."

In that case you are fortunate, for if you are as far down as you can get there is no further down you can go. There is only one direction you can take from this position, and that is up. So your situation is quite encouraging. However, I caution you not to take the attitude that you are in a situation in which nobody has ever been before. There is no such situation.

Practically speaking, there are only a few human stories and they have all been enacted previously. This is a fact that you must never forget — there are people who have overcome every conceivable difficult situation, even the one in which you now find yourself and which to you seems utterly hopeless. So did it seem to some others, but they found an out, a way up, a path over, a pass through.

An effective method for making your subconscious positive in character is to eliminate certain expressions of thought and speech which we may call the "little negatives." These so-called "little negatives" clutter up the average person's conversation, and while each one is seemingly unimportant in itself, the total effect of these attitudes is to condition the mind negatively. When this thought of "little negatives" first occurred to me, I began to analyze my own conversational habits and was shocked by what I found. I discovered that I was making such statements as, "I'm afraid I'll be late," or "I wonder if I'll have a flat tire," or "I don't think I can do that," or "I'll never get through this job. There's so much to do." If something turned out badly, I might say, "Oh, that's just what I expected." Or, again, I might observe a few clouds in the sky and would gloomily state, "I knew it was going to rain."

These are "little negatives" to be sure, and a big thought is of course more powerful than a little one, but it must never be forgotten that "mighty oaks from little acorns grow," and if a mass of "little negatives" clutter up your conversation, they are bound to seep into your mind. It is surprising how they accumulate in force, and presently, before you know it, they will grow into "big negatives." So I determined to go to work on the "little negatives" and root them out of my conversation. I found that the best way to eliminate them was deliberately to say a positive word about everything. When you keep asserting that things are going to work out well, that you can do the job, that you will not have a flat tire, that you will get there on time, by talking good results you invoke the law of positive effects and good results occur. Things do turn out well.

So to overcome your obstacles and live the "I don't believe in defeat" philosophy, cultivate a positive-idea pattern deeply in your consciousness. What we do with obstacles is directly determined by our mental attitude. Most of our obstacles, as a matter of fact, are mental in charcter.

"Ah," you may object, "mine are not mental, mine are real."

Perhaps so, but your attitude toward them is mental. The only possible way you can have an attitude is by the mental process, and what you think about your obstacles largely determines what you do about them. Form the mental attitude that you cannot remove an obstacle and you will not remove it, not if you think you can't. But get the idea firmly fixed that the obstacle is not so great as you previously considered it to be. Hold the idea that it is removable, and however faintly you entertain this positive thought, from the very moment you begin to think in this manner, the process is inaugurated which will lead to its ultimate removal.

If you have been long defeated by a difficulty, it is probably because you have told yourself for weeks, months, and even for years that there is nothing you can do about it. You have so emphasized your inability to yourself that your mind gradually accepted the conclusion upon which you have insisted, and when your mind is convinced, you are convinced, for as you think so are you.

But, on the contrary, when you employ this new and creative concept, "I can do all things through Christ," then you develop a new mental slant. Emphasize and re-emphasize that positive attitude

47

and you will finally convince your own consciousness that you can do something about difficulties. When at last your mind becomes convinced, astonishing results will begin to happen. Of a sudden you discover that you have the power you would never acknowledge.

Your obstacles are present all right. They are not fanciful, but they are not actually so difficult as they seem. Your mental attitude is the most important factor. Believe that Almighty God has put in you the power to lift yourself out of the rough by keeping your eye firmly fixed on the source of your power. Affirm to yourself that through this power you can do anything you have to do. Believe that this power is taking the tension out of you, that this power is flowing through you. Believe this, and a sense of victory will come.

Now take another look at that obstacle that has been bothering you. You will find that it isn't so formidable as you thought. Say to yourself, "The rough is only mental. I think victory — I get victory." Remember that formula. Write it on a piece of paper, put it in your wallet, stick it up on your mirror where you shave each morning, put it over the kitchen sink, put it on your dressing table and on your desk — keep looking at it until its truth drives into the depths of your consciousness, until it permeates your whole mental attitude, until it becomes a positive obsession —- "I can do all things through Christ which strengtheneth me."

What may seem to be a difficult proposition is, as I have pointed out, hard or easy in proportion to how we think about it. It may be said that three men vitally affected the thought processes of Americans — Emerson, Thoreau, and William James. Analyze the American mind even to this late date and it is evident that the teachings of these three philosophers combined to create that particular genius of the American who is not defeated by obstacles and who accomplishes "impossibles" with amazing efficiency.

A fundamental doctrine of Emerson is that the human personality can be touched with Divine power and thus greatness can be released from it. William James pointed out that the greatest factor in any undertaking is one's belief about it. Thoreau told us that the secret of achievement is to hold a picture of a successful outcome in mind.

Still another wise American was Thomas Jefferson, who, like Franklin, set for his guidance a series of rules. Franklin had thirteen daily rules; Jefferson only ten. One of Jefferson's rules was this, and I think it is priceless, "Always take hold of things by the smooth handle." That is, go at a job or at your difficulty by the use of a method that will encounter the least resistance. Resistance causes friction in mechanics, therefore it is necessary in mechanics to overcome or reduce friction. The negative attitude is a friction approach. That is why negativism develops such great resistance. The positive approach is the "smooth handle" technique. It is in harmony with the flow of the universe. It not only encounters less resistance, but actually stimulates assistance forces. It is remarkable how from early life until the end of your earthly existence the application of this philosophy will enable you to attain successful results in areas where otherwise you would be defeated.

As you finish this chapter please say the following line aloud: "I don't believe in defeat." Continue to affirm that until the idea dominates your subconscious attitudes.

❧ 9 ❧

How To Break The Worry Habit

 You do not need to be a victim of worry. Reduced to its simplest form, what is worry? It is simply an unhealthy and destructive mental habit. You were not born with the worry habit. You acquired it. And because you can change any habit and any acquired attitude, you can cast worry from your mind. Since aggressive, direct action is essential in the elimination process, there is just one proper time to begin an effective attack on worry, and that is now. So let us start breaking your worry habit at once.

Why should we take the worry problem this seriously? The reason is clearly stated by Dr. Smiley Blanton, eminent psychiatrist, "Anxiety is the great modern plague."

A famous psychologist asserts that "fear is the most disintegrating enemy of human personality," and a prominent physician declares that "worry is the most subtle and destructive of all human diseases." Another physician tells us that thousands of people are ill because of "dammed-up anxiety." These sufferers have been unable to expel their anxieties which have turned inward on the personality, causing many forms of ill-health. The destructive quality of worry is indicated by the fact that the word itself is derived from an old Anglo-Saxon word meaning "to choke." If someone were to put his fingers around your throat and press hard, cutting off the flow of vital power, it would be a dramatic demonstration of what you do to yourself by long-held and habitual worry.

We are told that worry is not infrequently a factor in arthritis. Physicians who have analyzed the causes of this prevalent disease assert that the following factors, at least some of them, are nearly always present in arthritic cases: financial disaster, frustration, tension, apprehension, loneliness, grief, long-held ill will, and habitual worry.

A clinic staff is said to have made a study of one hundred seventy-six American executives of the average age of forty-four years and discovered that one half had high blood pressure, heart disease, or ulcers. It was notable in every case of those thus afflicted that worry was a prominent factor.

The worrier, so it seems, is not likely to live as long as the person who learns to overcome his worries. The *Rotarian* magazine carried an article entitled "How Long Can You Live?" The author says that the waistline is the measure of your life line. The article also declares that if you want to live long, observe the following rules: (1) Keep calm. (2) Go to church. (3) Eliminate worry.

A survey shows that church members live longer than non-church members (better join the church if you don't want to die young). Married people, according to the article, live longer than single people. Perhaps this is because a married couple can divide the worry. When you are single, you have to do it all alone.

A scientific expert on length of life made a study of some 450 people who lived to be one hundred years of age. He found that these people lived long and contented lives for the following reasons: (1) They kept busy. (2) They used moderation in all things. (3) They ate lightly and simply. (4) They got a great deal of fun out of life. (5) They were early to bed and early up. (6) They were free from worry and fear, especially fear of death. (7) They had serene minds and faith in God.

Haven't you often heard a person say, "I am almost sick with worry," and then add with a laugh, "But I guess worry never really makes you ill." But that is where he is wrong. Worry can make you ill.

Dr. George W. Crile, famous American surgeon, said, "We fear not only in our minds but in our hearts, brains, and viscera, that whatever the cause of fear and worry, the effect can always be noted in the cells, tissues, and organs of the body."

Dr. Stanley Cobb, neurologist, says that worry is intimately connected with the symptoms of rheumatoid arthritis.

A doctor recently stated that there is an epidemic of fear and worry in this country. "All doctors," he declared, "are having cases of illness which are brought on directly by fear, and aggravated by worry and a feeling of insecurity."

But do not be discouraged, for you can overcome your worries. There is a remedy that will bring you sure relief. It can help you break the worry habit. And the first step to take in breaking it is simply to believe that you can. Whatever you believe you can do, you can do, with God's help.

Here, then, is a practical procedure which will help to eliminate abnormal worry from your experience.

Practice emptying the mind daily. This should be done preferably before retiring at night to avoid the retention by the consciousness of worries while you sleep. During sleep, thoughts tend to sink more deeply into the subconscious. The last five minutes before going to sleep are of extraordinary importance, for in that brief period the mind is most receptive to suggestion. It tends to absorb the last ideas that are entertained in waking consciousness.

This process of mind drainage is important in overcoming worry, for fear thoughts, unless drained off, can clog the mind and impede the flow of mental and spiritual power. But such thoughts can be emptied from the mind and will not accumulate if they are eliminated daily. To drain them, utilize a process of creative imagination. Conceive of yourself as actually emptying your mind of all anxiety and fear. Picture all worry thoughts as flowing out as you would let water flow from a basin by removing the stopper. Repeat the following affirmation during this visualization: "With God's help I am now emptying my mind of all anxiety, all fear, all sense of insecurity." Repeat this slowly five times, then add, "I believe that my mind is now emptied of all anxiety, all fear, all sense of insecurity." Repeat that statement five times, meanwhile holding a a mental picture of your mind as being emptied of these concepts. Then thank God for thus freeing you from fear. Then go to sleep.

In starting the curative process the foregoing method should be utilized in midmorning and midafternoon as well as at bedtime. Go into some quiet place for five minutes for this purpose. Faithfully perform this process and you will soon note beneficial results.

The procedure may be further strengthened by imaginatively thinking of yourself as reaching into your mind and one by one removing your worries. A small child possesses an imaginative skill superior to that of adults. A child responds to the game of kissing away a hurt or throwing away a fear. This simple process works for the child because in his mind he believes that that is actually the end of it. The dramatic act is a fact for him and so it proves to be the end of the matter. Visualize your fears as being drained out of your mind and the visualization will in due course be actualized.

Imagination is a source of fear, but imagination may also be the cure of fear. "Imagineering" is the use of mental images to build factual results, and it is an astonishingly effective procedure. Imagination is not simply the use of fancy. The word imagination derives from the idea of imaging. That is to say, you form an image either of fear or of release from fear. What you "image" (imagine) may ultimately become a fact if held mentally with sufficient faith.

Therefore hold an image of yourself as delivered from worry

53

and the drainage process will in time eliminate abnormal fear from your thoughts. However, it is not enough to empty the mind, for the mind, will not long remain empty. It must be occupied by something. It cannot continue in a state of vacuum. Therefore, upon emptying the mind, practice refilling it. Fill it with thoughts of faith, hope, courage, expectancy. Say aloud such affirmations as the following: "God is now filling my mind with courage, with peace, with calm assurance. God is now protecting me from all harm. God is now protecting my loved ones from all harm. God is now guiding me to right decisions. God will see me through this situation."

A half-dozen times each day crowd your mind with such thoughts as these until the mind is overflowing with them. In due course these thoughts of faith will crowd out worry. Fear is the most powerful of all thoughts with one exception, and that one exception is faith. Faith can always overcome fear. Faith is the one power against which fear cannot stand. Day by day, as you fill your mind with faith, there will ultimately be no room left for fear. This is the one great fact that no one should forget. Master faith and you will automatically master fear.

So the process is — empty the mind and cauterize it with God's grace, then practice filling your mind with faith and you will break the worry habit.

Fill your mind with faith and in due course the accumulation of faith will crowd out fear. It will not be of much value merely to read this suggestion unless you practice it. And the time to begin practicing it is now while you think of it and while you are convinced that the number-one procedure in breaking the worry habit is to drain the mind daily of fear and fill the mind daily with faith. It is just as simple as that. Learn to be a practicer of faith until you become an expert in faith. Then fear cannot live in you.

The importance of freeing your mind of fear cannot be overemphasized. Fear something over a long period of time and there is a real possibility that by fearing you may actually help bring it to pass. The Bible contains a line which is one of the most terrible statements ever made — terrible in its truth: "For the thing which I greatly feared is come upon me . . ." (Job 3:25) Of course it will, for if you fear something continuously you tend to create conditions in your mind propitious to the development of that which you fear. An atmosphere is encouraged in which it can take root and grow. You tend to draw it to yourself.

But do not be alarmed. The Bible also constantly reiterates another great truth, "That which I have greatly believed has come upon me." It does not make that statement in so many words, and yet again and again and still again the Bible tells us that if we have faith "nothing is impossible" unto us, and "according to your faith be it done unto you." So if you shift your mind from fear to faith you will stop creating the object of your fear and will, instead, actualize the object of your faith. Surround your mind with healthy thoughts, thoughts of faith, and not fear, and you will produce faith results instead of fear results.

Strategy must be used in the campaign against the worry habit. A frontal attack on the main body of worry with the expectation of conquering it may prove difficult. Perhaps a more adroit plan is to conquer the outer fortifications one by one, gradually closing in on the main position.

To change the figure, it might be well to snip off the little worries on the farthest branches of your fear. Then work back and finally destroy the main trunk of worry.

Worry is a destructive process of occupying the mind with thoughts contrary to God's love and care. Basically that is all worry is. The cure is to fill the mind with thoughts of God's power, His protection, and His goodness. So spend fifteen minutes daily filling your mind full of God. Cram your mind full of the "I believe philosophy," and you will have no mental room left to accommodate thoughts of worry and lack of faith.

The secret is to work out a method of attack and keep working at it. There is value in doing something that dramatizes to our own minds that an effective counterattack is in process. In so doing we bring spiritual forces to bear upon the problem in a manner both understandable and usable.

To conclude this chapter in a manner designed to help you go to work *now* to break the worry habit, I list a ten-point worry-breaking formula.

❧**1.** Say to yourself, "Worry is just a very bad mental habit. And I can change any habit with God's help."

❧**2.** You became a worrier by practicing worry. You can become free of worry by practicing the opposite and stronger habit of faith. With all the strength and perseverance you can command, start practicing faith.

❧**3.** How do you practice faith? First thing every morning before you arise say out loud, "I believe," three times.

❧**4.** Pray, using this formula, "I place this day, my life, my loved ones, my work in the Lord's hands. There is no harm in the Lord's hands, only good. Whatever happens, whatever results, if I am in the Lord's hands it is the Lord's will and it is good."

❧**5.** Practice saying something positive concerning everything about which you have been talking negatively. Talk positively. For example, don't say, "This is going to be a terrible day." Instead, affirm, "This is going to be a glorious day." Don't say, "I'll never be able to do that." Instead, affirm, "With God's help I will do that."

❧**6.** Never participate in a worry conversation. Shoot an injection of faith into all your conversations. A group of people talking pessimistically can infect every person in the group with negativism. But by talking things up rather than down you can drive off that depressing atmosphere and make everyone feel hopeful and happy.

❧**7.** One reason you are a worrier is that your mind is literally saturated with apprehension thoughts, defeat thoughts, gloomy thoughts. To counteract, mark every passage in the Bible that speaks of faith, hope, happiness, glory, radiance. Commit each to memory. Say them over and over again until these creative thoughts saturate your subconscious mind. Then the subconscious will return to you what you have given it, namely, optimism, not worry.

❧ **8.** Cultivate friendships with hopeful people. Surround yourself with friends who think positive, faith-producing thoughts and who contribute to a creative atmosphere. This will keep you restimulated with faith attitudes.

❧ **9.** See how many people you can help to cure their own worry habit. In helping another to overcome worry you get greater power over it within yourself.

❧ **10.** Every day of your life conceive of yourself as living in partnership and companionship with Jesus Christ. If He actually walked by your side, would you be worried or afraid? Well, then, say to yourself, "He is with me." Affirm aloud, "I am with you always." Then change it to say, "He is with me now." Repeat that affirmation three times every day.

✺〔 10 〕✺

Power To Solve Personal Problems

An effective technique in problem solving is the simple device of conceiving of God as a partner. One of the basic truths taught by the Bible is that God is with us. In fact, Christianity begins with that concept, for when Jesus Christ was born He was called Immanuel, meaning "God with us."

Christianity teaches that in all the difficulties, problems, and circumstances of this life God is close by. We can talk to Him, lean upon Him, get help from Him, and have the inestimable benefit of His interest, support and help. Practically everybody believes in a general way that this is true, and many have experienced the reality of this faith.

In getting correct solutions to your problems, however, it is necessary to go a step further than believing this, for one must actually practice the idea of presence. Practice believing that God is as real and actual as your wife, or your business partner, or your closest friend. Practice talking matters over with Him; believe that He hears and gives thought to your problem. Assume that He impresses upon your mind through consciousness the proper ideas and insights necessary to solve your problems. Definitely believe that in these solutions there will be no error, but that you will be guided to actions according to truth which results in right outcomes.

I cannot emphasize too strongly the effectiveness of this technique of problem solving. It has produced amazing results in the many cases coming under my observation.

In the very necessary business of solving personal problems, it is important, first of all, to realize that the power to solve them correctly is inherent within you. Second, it is necessary to work out and actualize a plan. Spiritual and emotional planlessness is a definite reason for the failure of many people to meet their personal problems successfully.

A business executive told me that he puts his dependence upon the "emergency powers of the human brain." It is his theory, and a sound one, that a human being possesses extra powers that may be tapped and utilized under emergency situations. In the ordinary conduct of day-by-day living, these emergency powers lie dormant, but under extraordinary circumstances the personality is able, when called upon, to deliver extra power if needed.

A person who develops a working faith does not allow these powers to lie dormant, but in proportion to his faith brings many of them into play in connection with normal activity. This explains why some people demonstrate greater force than others in daily requirements and in a crisis. They have made it a habit normally to draw upon powers that would otherwise be ignored except in some dramatic necessity.

When a difficult situation arises, do you know how to meet it? Have you any clearly defined plan for solving unusually difficult problems as they develop? Many people proceed on a hit-or-miss method, and, sadly enough, most frequently they miss. I cannot urge too strongly the importance of a planned use of your greater powers in meeting problems.

In addition to the method of two or three praying together in the "surrender of God" technique and that of establishing a partnership with God and the importance of a plan to tap and utilize emergency inner powers, there is still another tremendous technique — that of practicing faith attitudes. I read the Bible for years before it ever dawned on me that it was trying to tell me that if I would have faith — and really have it — that I could overcome all of my difficulties, meet every situation, rise above every defeat, and solve all of the perplexing problems of my life. The day that realization dawned on me was one of the greatest, if not the greatest, of my life. Undoubtedly many people will read this book who have never gotten the faith idea of living. But I hope you will get it now, for the faith technique is without question one of the most powerful truths in the world having to do with the successful conduct of human life.

Throughout the Bible the truth is emphasized again and again that "If ye have faith as a grain of mustard seed . . . nothing shall be impossible unto you." (Matthew 17:20) The Bible means this absolutely, factually, completely, and literally. It isn't an illusion, it isn't a fantasy. It is not an illustration, nor a symbol, nor a metaphor, but the absolute fact — "Faith, even as a grain of mustard seed," will solve your problems, any of your problems, all of your problems, if you believe it and practice it. "According to your faith, be it unto you." (Matthew 9:29) The requirement is faith, and directly in proportion to the faith that you have and use will you get results. Little faith gives you little results, medium faith gives you medium results, great faith gives you great results. But in the generosity of Almighty God, if you have only the faith symbolized by a grain of mustard seed, it will do amazing things in solving your problems.

In this chapter I have tried to show various methods for solving a problem. Now I wish to give ten simple suggestions as a concrete technique to use generally in solving your problems:

❧ **1.** Believe that for every problem there is a solution.

❧ **2.** Keep calm. Tension blocks the flow of thought power. Your brain cannot operate efficiently under stress. Go at your problem easy-like.

3. Don't try to force an answer. Keep your mind relaxed so that the solution will open up and become clear.

4. Assemble all the facts impartially, impersonally, and judicially.

5. List these facts on paper. This clarifies your thinking, bringing the various elements into orderly system. You see as well as think. The problem becomes objective, not subjective.

6. Pray about your problem, affirming that God will flash illumination into your mind.

7. Believe in and seek God's guidance on the promise of the 73rd Psalm, "Thou wilt guide me by thy counsel."

8. Trust in the faculty of insight and intuition.

9. Go to church and let your subconscious work on the problem as you attune to the mood of worship. Creative spiritual thinking has amazing power to give "right" answers.

10. If you follow these steps faithfully, then the answer that develops in your mind, or comes to pass, is the right answer to your problem.

❧ 11 ❧

How To Use Faith In Healing

 Is religious faith a factor in healing? Important evidence indicates that it is. There was a time in my own experience when I was not convinced of this, but now I am, and that very definitely. I have seen too many evidences to believe otherwise.

We are learning that faith properly understood and applied is a powerful factor in overcoming disease and establishing health.

There is a growing emphasis in present-day religious practice which is designed to help people find healing from the sicknesses of mind, heart, soul, and body. This is a return to the original practice of Christianity. Only in recent times have we tended to overlook the fact that for centuries religion carried on healing activities. The very word "pastor" derives from a word meaning "the cure of souls." In modern times, however, man made the false assumption that it is impossible to harmonize the teachings of the Bible with what is called "science" and so the healing emphasis of religion was abandoned almost entirely to materialistic science. Today, however, the close association of religion and health is increasingly recognized.

It is significant that the word "holiness" derives from a word meaning "wholeness" and the word "meditation," usually used in a religious sense, closely resembles the root meaning of the word "medication." The affinity of the two words is startlingly evident when we realize that sincere and practical meditation upon God and His truth acts as a medication for the soul and body.

Present-day medicine emphasizes psychosomatic factors in healing, thus recognizing the relationship of mental states to bodily health. Modern medical practice realizes and takes into consideration the close connection between how a man thinks and how he feels. Since religion deals with thought and feeling and basic attitudes, it is only natural that the science of faith should be important in the healing process.

A sensible and effective pattern for health and happiness is to utilize the skills and methods of medical science to the fullest possible extent and at the same time apply the wisdom, the experience, and the techniques of spiritual science. There is impressive evidence to support the belief that God works through both the practitioner of science, the doctor, and the practitioner of faith, the minister. Many physicians join in this point of view.

Years ago my friend, Dr. Clarence W. Lieb, pointed out to me the effect on health of spiritual and psychiatric problems, and through his wise guidance I began to see that fear and guilt, hate and resentment, problems with which I was dealing, were often closely connected with problems of health and physical well-being. So profoundly does Dr. Lieb believe in this therapy that he with Dr. Smiley Blanton inaugurated the religio-psychiatric clinic which for years has ministered to hundreds at the Marble Collegiate Church in New York.

The late Dr. William Seaman Bainbridge and I worked closely together in the relationship of religion and surgery, and we were able to bring health and new life to many.

Two of my medical friends in New York, Dr. Z. Taylor Bercovitz and Dr. Howard Westcott, have been of inestimable help in my pastoral work through their wisely scientific and yet deeply spiritual understanding of the ills of the body, mind, and soul as related to faith.

In the light of this viewpoint based on a strictly common-sense scientific attitude we may approach the phenomenon of healing through faith with credibility. If I did not believe sincerely that the faith factor in healing is sound I would certainly not develop the point of view contained in this chapter.

Over a period of time I have received from many readers and radio listeners as well as from my own parishioners accounts of healings in which the element of faith has been present. I have meticulously investigated many of these to satisfy my own mind as to their truthfulness. Also I wanted to be able to declare to the most cynical that here is a way of health, happiness, and successful living which is so buttressed by evidence that only the person who wants to remain ill because of some subconscious will-to-fail attitude will ignore his possibilities for health implied in these experiences.

The formula which these many incidents together present is briefly stated — the employment of all the resources of medical and psychological science combined with the resources of spiritual science. This is a combination of therapies that can surely bring health and well-being if it is the plan of God for the patient to live. Obviously for each of us there comes a time for this mortal life to end (life itself never ends, only the earthly phase of it).

We in the so-called old-line churches have, in my humble judgment, missed one of our greatest possible contributions by failing to point out with positiveness that there is a sound message of health in Christianity. Failing to find this emphasis in the church, groups, organizations, and other spiritual bodies have been created to supply this deficiency in Christian teaching. But there is no longer any valid reason why all the churches should not recognize that which is authenticated, namely, that there is healing in faith and more generally offer sound healing techniques to our people. Fortunately everywhere today throughout our religious organizations thoughtful, scientifically minded spiritual leaders are taking that extra step of faith based on the facts (and the Scripture) and are making available to the people as never before the formulas of the marvelous healing grace of Jesus Christ.

In all of the investigations I have made into successful cases of healing, there seem to be certain factors present. First, a complete willingness to surrender oneself into the hands of God. Second, a complete letting go of all error such as sin in any form and a desire to be cleansed in the soul. Third, belief and faith in the combined therapy of medical science in harmony with the healing power of God. Fourth, a sincere willingness to accept God's answer, whatever it may be, and no irritation or bitterness against His will. Fifth, a substantial, unquestioning faith that God can heal.

In all these healings there seems to be an emphasis upon warmth and light and a feeling of assurance that power has passed through. In practically every case that I have examined, in one form or another, the patient talks about a moment when there was warmth, heat, beauty, peace, joy, and a sense of release. Sometimes it has been a sudden experience; other times a more gradual unfolding of the conviction that the healing has occurred.

Always in my investigation of these matters I have waited for elapsed time to prove that the healing is permanent and those cases are not based on any temporary improvement which might conceivably be the result of a momentary resurgence of strength.

In many heart cases the therapy of faith (a quiet, serene faith in Jesus Christ) undoubtedly stimulates healing. People who experience "a heart attack" who thereupon thoroughly and completely practice faith in Christ's healing grace, observing at the same time the rules prescribed by their physicians, report remarkable recovery histories. Perhaps such a person may even gain a greater degree of health than previously for having learned his limitations and, realizing the excess strains he has been placing upon himself, now conserves his strength.

But more than that he has learned one of the greatest techniques of human well-being, that of surrendering himself to the recuperative power of God. This is done by consciously attaching himself to the creative process through mentally conceiving of re-creative forces as operating within himself. The patient opens his consciousness to the tides of vitality and re-creative energy inherent in the universe which have been barred from his life through tension, high pressure, and other departures from the laws of well-being.

In the prevention of sickness and in healing mind and body, do not fail to draw upon one of the greatest resources available to you — the faith that heals.

In the light of the principles outlined in this chapter, what can you do of a constructive nature when a loved one or you are ill? Following are eight practical suggestions:

❧ **1.** Follow the advice of a prominent medical school head who said, "In sickness, send for your minister even as you send for your doctor." In other words, believe that spiritual forces as well as medical technique are important in healing.

❧ **2.** Pray for the doctor. Realize that God uses trained human instrumentality to aid His healing powers. As one doctor has put it, "We treat the patient and God heals him." Pray, therefore, that the doctor may be an open channel of God's healing grace.

❧ **3.** Whatever you do, do not become panicky or filled with fear, for if you do, you will send out negative thoughts and therefore destructive thoughts in the direction of your loved one when he requires positive and healing thoughts to assist him.

❧ **4.** Remember that God does nothing except by law. Also remember that our little materialistic laws are only fragmentary revelations of the great power flowing through the universe. Spiritual law also governs illness. God has arranged two remedies for all illness. One is healing through natural laws applicable by science, and the other brings healing by spiritual law applicable through faith.

❧**5.** Completely surrender your loved one into the hands of God. By your faith you can place him in the flow of Divine power. There is healing there, but in order for it to be effective the patient must be completely released to the operation of God's will. This is difficult to understand and equally difficult to perform, but it is a fact that if the great desire for the loved one to live is matched with an equally great willingness to relinquish him to God, healing powers are amazingly set in motion.

❧**6.** It is also important that harmony prevail in the family, that is, a spiritual harmony. Remember the emphasis in the scripture, Matthew 18:19: "If two of you shall agree on earth as touching anything that they shall ask, it shall be done for them of my Father which is in heaven." Apparently disharmony and disease are akin.

❧**7.** Form a picture in your mind of the loved one as being well. Visualize him in perfect health. Picture him as radiant with the love and goodness of God. The conscious mind may suggest sickness, even death, but nine tenths of your mind is in the subconscious. Let the picture of health sink into the subconscious and this powerful part of your mind will send forth radiant health energy. What we believe in the subconscious we usually get. Unless your faith controls the subconscious, you will never get any good thing, for the subconscious gives back only that which your real thought is. If the real thought is negative, the results will also be negative. If the real thought is positive, you will get positive and healing results.

❧**8.** Be perfectly natural. Ask God to heal your loved one. That is what you want with all your heart, so ask Him please to do it, but we suggest that you say PLEASE just once. Thereafter in your prayer, thank Him for His goodness. This affirmative faith will help to release deep spiritual power and also joy through reassurance of God's loving care. This joy will sustain you, and remember that joy itself possesses healing power.

❧ 12 ❧

When Vitality Sags,
Try This Health Formula

 A woman, so I have heard, went into a drugstore and asked for a bottle of psychosomatic medicine.

Such medicine, of course, is not found on drugstore shelves for it does not come in pills or bottles. But there is a psychosomatic medicine just the same and many of us need it. It is a prescription compounded of prayer, faith, and dynamic spiritual thinking.

It has been variously computed that from 50 to 75 per cent of present-day people are ill because of the influence of improper mental states on their emotional and physical make-up. Therefore such a medicine is of great importance. Many people who are below par will find that there is a health formula which, in addition to the services of their physicians, can be of great value to them.

Every thoughtful person who has ever considered the matter realizes that the doctors are right when they tell us that resentment, hate, grudge, ill will, jealousy, vindictiveness, are attitudes which produce ill-health. Have a fit of anger and experience for yourself that sinking feeling in the pit of your stomach, that sense of stomach sickness. Chemical reactions in the body are set up by emotional outbursts that result in feelings of ill-health. Should these be continued either violently or in a simmering state over a period of time, the general condition of the body will deteriorate.

So we realize today the effect of thought patterns upon physical states. We realize that a person can make himself ill by resentment. We know he can develop various kinds of physiological symptoms because of a sense of guilt. Also one may show definite physical symptoms as a result of fear and anxiety. We know that healing has been accomplished when the thoughts are changed.

I was interested to read a statement by a psychologist that infants can "catch" fear and hatred from people around them more quickly than they can catch measles or other infectious diseases. The virus of fear may burrow deeply into their subconsciousness and remain there for a lifetime. "But," adds the psychologist, "fortunately infants can also catch love and goodness and faith and so grow up to become normal, healthy children and adults."

In an article in the *Ladies' Home Journal*, Constance J. Foster quotes Dr. Edward Weiss of Temple University Medical School in a speech to the American College of Physicians in which Dr. Weiss stated that chronic victims of pains and aches in the muscles and joints may be suffering from nursing a smoldering grudge against someone close to them. He added that such persons usually are totally unaware that they bear a chronic resentment.

"To clear up any possible misunderstanding," the author continues, "it is necessary to state emphatically that emotions and feelings are quite as real as germs and no less respectable. The resultant pain and suffering of diseases caused primarily by the emotions are no more imaginary than those caused by bacteria. In no case is the patient consciously to blame for developing the disease. Such persons are not suffering from any disease of the mind, but rather from a disorder of their feelings, often linked to a marital or parent-child problem."

And yet people still think that when the Bible tells you not to hate or to get angry that it is "theoretical advice." The Bible is not theoretical. It is our greatest book of wisdom. It is filled with practical advice on living and on health. Anger, resentment, and guilt make you sick, modern physicians tell us, which proves once again that the most up-to-date book on personal well-being is the Holy Bible, neglected by so many or regarded by them as purely a religious book and certainly as one that is not practical. No wonder more copies are read than all other books. That is because in this book we discover not only what is wrong with us but how to correct it as well.

Since irritation, anger, hate, and resentment have such a powerful effect in producing ill-health, what is the antidote? Obviously it is to fill the mind with attitudes of good will, forgiveness, faith, love, and the spirit of imperturbability. And how is that accomplished? Following are some practical suggestions. They have been used successfully by many in counterattacking especially the emotion of anger. A consistent application of these suggestions can produce feelings of well-being:

❧ **1.** Remember that anger is an emotion, and an emotion is always warm, even hot. Therefore to reduce an emotion, cool it. And how do you cool it? When a person gets angry, the fists tend to clench, the voice rises in stridency, muscles tense, the body becomes rigid. (Psychologically you are poised for fight, adrenalin shoots through the body.) This is the old caveman hangover in the nervous system. So deliberately oppose the heat of this emotion with coolness — freeze it out. Deliberately, by an act of will, keep your hands from clenching. Hold your fingers out straight. Deliberately reduce your tone; bring it down to a whisper. Remember that it is difficult to argue in a whisper. Slump in a chair, or even lie down if possible. It is very difficult to get mad lying down.

❧ **2.** Say aloud to yourself, "Don't be a fool. This won't get me anywhere, so skip it." At that moment it may be a bit hard to pray, but try it anyway; at least conjure up a picture of Jesus Christ in your mind and try to think of Him mad just as you are. You can't do it, and the effort will serve to puncture your angry emotions.

70

3. One of the best techniques for cooling off anger was suggested by Mrs. Grace Oursler. She formerly employed the usual "count to ten" technique but happened to notice that the first ten words of the Lord's Prayer worked better. "Our Father who art in Heaven, hallowed be Thy name." When angry, say that ten times and your anger will lose its power over you.

4. Anger is a great term expressing the accumulated vehemence of a multitude of minor irritations. These irritations, each rather small in itself, having gathered force by reason of the one being added to the other, finally blaze forth in a fury that often leaves us abashed at ourselves. Therefore, make a list of everything that irritates you. No matter how inconsequential it may be or how silly each is, list it just the same. The purpose in doing this is to dry up the tiny rivulets that feed the great river of anger.

5. Make each separate irritation a special object of prayer. Get a victory over each, one at a time. Instead of attempting to destroy all of your anger, which as we have pointed out is a consolidated force, snip away by prayer each annoyance that feeds your anger. In this way you will weaken your anger to the point where presently you will gain control over it.

6. Train yourself so that every time you feel the surge of anger you say, "Is this really worth what it is doing to me emotionally? I will make a fool of myself. I will lose friends." In order to get the full effect of this technique, practice saying to yourself a few times every day, "It is never worth it to get worked up or mad about anything." Also affirm: "It isn't worth it to spend $1000 worth of emotion on a five-cent irritation."

7. When a hurt-feeling situation arises, get it straightened out as quickly as possible. Don't brood over it for a minute longer than you can help. Do something about it. Do not allow yourself to sulk or indulge in self-pity. Don't mope around with resentful thoughts. The minute your feelings are hurt, do just as when you hurt your finger. Immediately apply the cure. Unless you do so the situation can become distorted out of all proportion. So put some spiritual iodine on the hurt at once by saying a prayer of love and forgiveness.

❖ **8.** Apply grievance drainage to your mind. That is, open your mind and let the grievance flow out. Go to someone you trust and pour it out to him until not a vestige of it remains within you. Then forget it.

❖ **9.** Simply start praying for the person who has hurt your feelings. Continue this until you feel the malice fading away. Sometimes you may have to pray for quite a while to get that result. A man who tried this method told me that he kept account of the number of times he needed to pray until the grievance left and peace came. It was exactly sixty-four times. He literally prayed it out of his system. This is positively guaranteed to work.

❖ **10.** Say this little prayer: "May the love of Christ fill my heart." Then add this line: "May the love of Christ for ——— (insert the other's name) flood my soul." Pray this, mean it (or ask to mean it), and you will get relief.

❖ **11.** Actually take the advice of Jesus to forgive seventy times seven. To be literal, that means four hundred ninety times. Before you have forgiven a person that many times you will be free of resentment.

❖ **12.** Finally, this wild, undisciplined, primitive urge in you which flames to the surface can be tamed only by allowing Jesus Christ to take control. Therefore, complete this lesson by saying to Jesus Christ, "Even as You can convert a person's morals, so now I ask You to convert my nerves. As You give power over the sins of the flesh, so give me power over the sins of the disposition. Bring my temper under Your control. Give me Thy healing peace in my nervous system as well as in my soul." If you are beset by temper, repeat the above prayer three times every day. It might be advisable to print it on a card and put it on your desk, or above the kitchen sink, or in your pocketbook.

Inflow Of New Thoughts Can Remake You

 One of the most important and powerful facts about you is expressed in the following statement by William James, who was one of the very few wisest men America has produced. William James said, "The greatest discovery of my generation *is that human beings can alter their lives by altering their attitudes of mind.*" As you think, so shall you be. So flush out all old, tired, worn-out thoughts. Fill your mind with fresh, new creative thoughts of faith, love, and goodness. By this process you can actually remake your life.

And where do you find such personality remaking thoughts?

It has been said that the wisest man who ever lived in America was Ralph Waldo Emerson, the Sage of Concord. Emerson declared, "A man is what he thinks about all day long."

A famous psychologist says, "There is a deep tendency in human nature to become precisely like that which you habitually imagine yourself to be."

It has been said that thoughts are things, that they actually possess dynamic power. Judged by the power they exercise one can readily accept such an appraisal. You can actually think yourself into or out of situations. You can make yourself ill with your thoughts and by the same token you can make yourself well by the use of a different and healing type of thought. Think one way and you attract the conditions which that type of thinking indicates. Think another way and you can create an entirely different set of conditions. Conditions are created by thoughts far more powerfully than conditions create thoughts.

Think positively, for example, and you set in motion positive forces which bring positive results to pass. Positive thoughts create around yourself an atmosphere propitious to the development of positive outcomes. On the contrary, think negative thoughts and you create around yourself an atmosphere propitious to the development of negative results.

To change your circumstances, first start thinking differently. Do not passively accept unsatisfactory circumstances, but form a picture in your mind of circumstances as they should be. Hold that picture, develop it firmly in all details, believe in it, pray about it, work at it, and you can actualize it according to that mental image emphasized in your positive thinking.

This is one of the greatest laws in the universe. Fervently do I wish I had discovered it as a very young man. It dawned upon me much later in life and I have found it to be one of the greatest if not my greatest discovery, outside of my relationship to God. And in a deep sense this law is a factor in one's relationship with God because it channels God's power into personality.

This great law briefly and simply stated is that if you think in negative terms you will get negative results. If you think in positive terms you will achieve positive results. That is the simple fact which is at the basis of an astonishing law of prosperity and success. In three words: Believe and succeed.

It is as simple as this — put your problem in God's hands. In your thoughts rise above the problem so that you look down upon it, not up at it. Test it according to God's will. That is, do not try to get success from something that is wrong. Be sure it is right morally, spiritually, and ethically. You can never get a right result from an error. If your thinking is wrong, it is wrong and not right and can never be right so long as it is wrong. If it is wrong in the essence it is bound to be wrong in the result.

Therefore be sure it is right, then hold it up in God's name and visualize a great result. Keep the idea of prosperity, of achievement, and of attainment firmly fixed in your mind. Never entertain a failure thought. Should a negative thought of defeat come into your mind, expel it by increasing the positive affirmation. Affirm aloud, "God is now giving me success. He is now giving me attainment." The mental vision which you create and firmly hold in consciousness will be actualized if you continually affirm it in your thoughts and if you work diligently and effectively. This creative process simply stated is: visualize, prayerize, and finally actualize.

People in all walks of life who accomplish notable achievements know the value of this law in their experience.

At this very minute, as you read this book, potential ideas are in your mind. By releasing and developing these ideas you can solve your financial problem, your business situation, you can care for yourself and your family, and attain success in your ventures. A steady inflow and practical use of these creative thoughts can remake your life and you along with it.

There was a time when I acquiesced in the silly idea that there is no relationship between faith and prosperity; that when one talked about religion he should never relate it to achievement, that it dealt only with ethics and morals or social values. But now I realize that such a viewpoint limits the power of God and the development of the individual. Religion teaches that there is a tremendous power in the universe and that this power can dwell in personality. It is a power that can blast out all defeat and lift a person above all difficult situations.

We have seen the demonstration of atomic energy. We know that astonishing and enormous energy exists in the universe. This same force of energy is resident in the human mind. Nothing on earth is greater than the human mind in potential power. The average individual is capable of much greater achievement than he has ever realized.

This is true regardless of who is reading this statement. When you actually learn to release yourself you will discover that your mind contains ideas of such creative value that you need not lack anything. By the full and proper use of your power stimulated by God power, you can make your life successful.

You can make just about anything of your life — anything you will believe or will visualize, anything you will pray for and work for. Look deeply into your mind. Amazing wonders are there.

Whatever your situation may be, you can improve it. First, quiet your mind so that inspirations may rise from its depths. Believe that God is now helping you. Visualize achievement. Organize your life on a spiritual basis so that God's principles work within you. Hold firmly in your mind a picture not of failure but of success. Do these things and creative thoughts will flow freely from your mind. This is an amazing law, one that can change anybody's life including your own. An inflow of new thoughts can remake you regardless of every difficulty you may now face, and I repeat — *every difficulty.*

In the last analysis the basic reason a person fails to live a creative and successful life is because of error within himself. He thinks wrong. He needs to correct the error in his thoughts. He needs to practice right thinking. When the 23rd Psalm says, "He leadeth me in the paths of righteousness," it not only means the paths of goodness, but the paths of right-mindedness as well. When Isaiah says, "Let the wicked forsake his way and the unrighteous man his thoughts," (Isaiah 55:7) it not only means that a person is to depart from evil and do good, but that he is to change his thinking from wrong to right, from error to truth. The great secret of successful living is to reduce the amount of error in oneself and increase the amount of truth. An inflow of new, right, health-laden thoughts through the mind creatively affects the circumstances of life, for truth always produces right procedures and therefore right results.

Following are seven practical step for changing your mental attitudes from negative to positive, for releasing creative new thoughts, and for shifting from error patterns to truth patterns. Try them — keep on trying them. They will work.

❧ **1.** For the next twenty-four hours, deliberately speak hopefully about everything, about your job, about your health, about your future. Go out of your way to talk optimistically about everything. This will be difficult, for possibly it is your habit to talk pessimistically. From this negative habit you must restrain yourself even if it requires an act of will.

❧ **2.** After speaking hopefully for twenty-four hours, continue the practice for one week, then you can be permitted to be "realistic" for a day or two. You will discover that what you meant by "realistic" a week ago was actually pessimistic, but what you now mean by "realistic" is something entirely different; it is the dawning of the positive outlook. When most people say they are being "realistic" they delude themselves: they are simply being negative.

❧ **3.** You must feed your mind even as you feed your body, and to make your mind healthy you must feed it nourishing, wholesome thoughts. Therefore, today start to shift your mind from negative to positive thinking. Start at the beginning of the New Testament and underscore every sentence about *Faith*. Continue doing this until you have marked every such passage in the four books, Matthew, Mark, Luke, and John. Particularly note Mark 11, verses 22, 23, 24. They will serve as samples of the verses you are to underscore and fix deeply in your consciousness.

❧ **4.** Then commit the underscored passages to memory. Commit one each day until you can recite the entire list from memory. This will take time, but remember you have consumed much more time becoming a negative thinker than this will require. Effort and time will be needed to unlearn your negative pattern.

➤ **5.** Make a list of your friends to determine who is the most positive thinker among them and deliberately cultivate his society. Do not abandon your negative friends, but get closer to those with a positive point of view for a while, until you have absorbed their spirit, then you can go back among your negative friends and give them your newly acquired thought pattern without taking on their negativism.

➤ **6.** Avoid argument, but whenever a negative attitude is expressed, counter with a positive and optimistic opinion.

➤ **7.** Pray a great deal and always let your prayer take the form of thanksgiving on the assumption that God is giving you great and wonderful things; for if you think He is, He surely is. God will not give you any greater blessing than you can believe in. He wants to give you great things, but even He cannot make you take anything greater than you are equipped by faith to receive. "According to your faith (that is, in proportion to) be it unto you." (Matthew 9:29)

The secret of a better and more successful life is to cast out those old dead, unhealthy thoughts. Substitute for them new vital, dynamic faith thoughts. You can depend upon it — an inflow of new thoughts will remake you and your life.

❊(14)❊

Relax For Easy Power

"Every night in these United States more than six million sleeping tablets are required to put the American people to sleep."

This startling statement was made to me several years ago by a drug manufacturer at a convention of that industry where I was giving a speech. Though his assertion seemed incredible, I have been told by others who are in a position to know that the above estimate is now an understatement.

In fact, I heard another good authority assert that the American people are using about twelve million doses of sleeping tablets per day. That is enough to put every twelfth American to sleep tonight. Statistics show that the use of sleeping tablets has risen 1000 per cent in recent years. But a more recent statement is even more startling. According to the vice-president of a large drug manufacturing concern approximately seven billion one-half-grain tablets are consumed yearly, which works out at about nineteen million tablets per night.

What a pathetic situation. Sleep is a natural restorative process. One would think that any person after a day's work would be able to sleep peacefully, but apparently Americans have even lost the art of sleeping. In fact, so keyed up are they that I, a minister with ample opportunity to test the matter, must report that the American people are so nervous and high-strung that now it is almost next to impossible to put them to sleep with a sermon. It has been years since I have seen anyone sleep in church. And that is a sad situation.

A Washington official who loves to juggle figures, especially astronomical figures, told me that last year in the United States there was a total of seven and a half billion headaches. This works itself out at approximately fifty headaches per head per annum. Have you had your quota yet this year? Just how this official arrived at these figures he did not say, but shortly after our conversation I noticed a report that in a recent year the drug industry sold eleven million pounds of aspirin. Perhaps this era might appropriately be termed "The Aspirin Age," as one author has called it.

An authoritative source declares that every other hospital bed in the United States is occupied by a patient who was put there not because he encountered a germ or had an accident or developed an organic malady, but because of his inability to organize and discipline his emotions.

In a clinic five hundred patients were examined hand running and 386, or 77 per cent, were found to be ill of psychosomatic difficulties — physical illness caused largely by unhealthy mental states. Another clinic made a study of a large number of ulcer cases and reported that nearly half were made ill, not as the result of physical troubles, but because the patients worried too much or hated too much, had too much guilt, or were tension victims.

A doctor from still another clinic made the observation that in his opinion medical men, despite all extraordinary scientific developments, are now able to heal by the means of science alone less than half the maladies brought them. He declares that in many cases patients are sending back into their bodies the diseased thoughts of their minds. Prominent among these diseased thoughts are anxiety and tension.

This unhappy situation has become so serious that in our own Marble Collegiate Church, Fifth Avenue at 29th Street, New York City, we now have twelve psychiatrists on the staff under the supervision of Dr. Smiley Blanton. Why psychiatrists on the staff of a church? The answer is that psychiatry is a science. Its function is the analysis, diagnosis, and treatment of human nature according to certain well-authenticated laws and procedures.

Christianity may also be thought of as a science. It is a philosophy, a system of theology, a system of metaphysics, and a system of worship. It also works itself out in moral and ethical codes. But Christianity also has the characteristics of a science in that it is based upon a book which contains a system of techniques and formulas designed for the understanding and treatment of human nature. The laws are so precise and have been so often demonstrated when proper conditions of understanding, belief, and practice are applied that religion may be said to form an exact science.

When a person comes to our clinic the first counselor is perhaps a psychiatrist who in a kindly and careful manner studies the problem and tells the patient "why he does what he does." This is a most important fact to learn. Why, for example, have you had an inferiority complex all your life long, or why have you been haunted by fear, or, again, why do you nurse resentment? Why have you always been shy and reticent, or why do you do stupid things or make inept statements? These phenomena of your human nature do not just happen. There is a reason why you do what you do and it is an important day in your life experience when at last you discover the reason. Self-knowledge is the beginning of self-correction.

Following the self-knowledge process the psychiatrist turns the patient over to the pastor who tells him how to do what he ought to do. The pastor applies to the case, in scientific and systematic form, the therapies of prayer, faith, and love. The psychiatrist and the minister pool their knowledge and combine their therapies with the result that many people have found new life and happiness. The minister does not attempt to be a psychiatrist nor the psychiatrist a pastor. Each performs his own function but always in co-operation.

The Christianity utilized in this procedure is the undiluted teachings of Jesus Christ, Lord and Saviour of man's life. We believe in the practical, absolute workability of the teachings of Jesus. We believe that we can indeed "do all things through Christ." (Philippians 4:13) The Gospel as we work with it proves to be a literal fulfillment of the astonishing promise, "Eye hath not seen, nor ear heard, neither have entered into the heart of man, the things which God hath prepared for them that love Him." (I Corinthians 2:9) Believe (in Christ); believe in His system of thought and practice; believe and you will overcome all fear, hate, inferiority, guilt, and every form and manner of defeat. In other words, no good thing is too good to be true. You have never seen, never heard, never even imagined the things God will give to those who love Him.

In the work of the clinic one frequent problem is that of tension. This, to a very large degree, may be called the prevailing malady of the American people. But not only the American people seem to suffer from tension. The Royal Bank of Canada some time ago devoted its monthly letter to this problem under the title, "Let's Slow Down," and says in part: "This monthly letter does not set itself up as a counselor of mental and physical health, but it is attempting to break down a problem that bedevils every adult person in Canada," and, I might add, in the United States as well.

The bank letter goes on to say: "We are victims of a mounting tension; we have difficulty in relaxing. Our high-strung nervous systems are on a perpetual binge. Caught up as we are in the rush all day, every day, and far into the night, we are not living fully. We must remember what Carlyle called 'the calm supremacy of the spirit over its circumstances.'"

When a prominent banking institution calls to the attention of its customers the fact that they are failing to derive from life what they really want from it because they have become victims of tension, it is certainly time something was done about the situation.

In St. Petersburg, Florida, I actually saw a machine on the street equipped with a sign, "What is your blood pressure?" You could put a coin in a slot and get the bad news. When you can buy a reading on blood pressure like you buy gum out of a slot machine, it indicates that many people have this problem.

One of the simplest methods for reducing tension is to practice the easy-does-it attitude. Do everything more slowly, less hectically, and without pressure. My friend Branch Rickey, famous baseball man, told me that he would not use a player no matter how well he hits, fields, or runs if he is guilty of "overpressing." To be a successful big-league baseball player there must be a flow of easy power through every action and of course through the mind. The most effective way to hit a ball is by the easy method, where all the muscles are flexible and operating in correlated power. Try to kill the ball and you will slice it or maybe miss it altogether. This is true in golf, in baseball, in every sport.

Of course I know a lot of lazy people who have been sittin' in the sun all their lives and never amounted to anything. There is a difference between sittin' and relaxing, and just sittin'. But if you sit and relax and think about God and get yourself in tune with Him and open yourself to the flow of His power, then sittin' is not laziness; in fact, it is about the best way to renew power. It produces driving energy, the kind of energy *you* drive, not the kind that drives you.

The secret is to keep the mind quiet, avoiding all hectic reactions of haste, and to practice peaceful thinking. The essence of the art is to keep the tempo down; to perform your responsibilities on the basis of the most efficient conservation of energy. It is advisable to adopt one or two workable plans through the use of which you can become expert in the practice of relaxed and easy power.

Relaxation results from re-creation, and the process of re-creation should be continuous. The human being is meant to be attached to a continual flow of force that proceeds from God through the individual and back to God for renewal. When one lives in tune with this constantly re-creative process he learns the indispensable quality to relax and work on the basis of easy does it.

Now, how to master this skill. Here are ten rules for taking the hard way out of your job. Try these proven methods for working hard easily. They will help you to relax and have easy power.

➤**1.** Don't get the idea that you are Atlas carrying the world on your shoulders. Don't strain so hard. Don't take yourself so seriously.

➤**2.** Determine to like your work. Then it will become a pleasure, not drudgery. Perhaps you do not need to change your job. Change yourself and your work will seem different.

➤**3.** Plan your work — work your plan. Lack of system produces that "I'm swamped" feeling.

➤**4.** Don't try to do everything at once. That is why time is spread out. Heed that wise advice from the Bible, "This one thing I do."

➤**5.** Get a correct mental attitude, remembering that ease or difficulty in your work depends upon how you think about it. Think it's hard and you make it hard. Think it's easy and it tends to become easy.

➤**6.** Become efficient in your work. "Knowledge is power" (over your job). It is always easier to do a thing right.

➤**7.** Practice being relaxed. Easy always does it. Don't press or tug. Take it in your stride.

❧ **8.** Discipline yourself not to put off until tomorrow what you can do today. Accumulation of undone jobs makes your work harder. Keep your work up to schedule.

❧ **9.** Pray about your work. You will get relaxed efficiency by so doing.

❧ **10.** Take on the "unseen partner." It is surprising the load He will take off you. God is as much at home in offices, factories, stores, kitchens, as in churches. He knows more about your job than you do. His help will make your work easy.

❊{ 15 }❊

How To Get People To Like You

We might as well admit it, we want people to like us.

You may hear someone say, "I don't care whether people like me or not." But whenever you hear anyone say that, just put it down as a fact that he is not really telling the truth.

The psychologist, William James, said, "One of the deepest drives of human nature is the desire to be appreciated." The longing to be liked, to be held in esteem, to be a sought-after person, is fundamental in us.

A poll was taken among some high-school students on the question, "What do you most desire?" By overwhelming majority the students voted that they wanted to be popular. The same urge is in older people as well. Indeed it is doubtful if anybody ever outlives the desire to be well thought of, to be highly regarded, or to have the affection of his associates.

To be master of the art of popularity, be artless. Strive deliberately after popularity and the chances are you will never attain it. But become one of those rare personalities about whom people say, "He certainly has something," and you can be certain you are on the way to having people like you.

I must warn you, however, that despite your attainments in popularity you will never get everybody to like you. There is a curious quirk in human nature whereby some people just naturally won't like you. A quatrain inscribed on a wall at Oxford says:

> *"I do not love thee, Dr. Fell,*
> *The reason why I cannot tell;*
> *But this alone I know full well,*
> *I do not love thee, Dr. Fell."*

That verse is very subtle. The author did not like Dr. Fell. He didn't know why but he just knew he didn't like him. It was most likely an unreasonable dislike, for undoubtedly Dr. Fell was a very nice person. Perhaps if the author had known him better he would have liked him, but poor Dr. Fell never did become popular with the author of those lines. It may have been due simply to a lack of *rapprochement,* that baffling mechanism by which we either do or do not "click" with certain people.

Even the Bible recognizes this unhappy fact about human nature, for it says, "If it be possible, as much as lieth in you, live peaceably with all men." (Romans 12:18) The Bible is a very realistic book and it knows people, their infinite possibilities as well as their imperfections. The Bible advised the disciples that if they went into a village and after trying their best to get along with people still couldn't do so, they were to shake off the very dust of the village from their feet — "And whosoever will not receive you, when ye go out of that city, shake off the very dust from your feet for a testimony against them." (Luke 9:5) This is all by way of saying that you will be wise if you do not let it too seriously affect you if you do not achieve perfect popularity with everyone.

However, there are certain formulas and procedures which, if followed faithfully, can make you a person whom other people like. You can enjoy satisfactory personal relationships even if you are a "difficult" person or by nature shy and retiring, even unsocial. You can make of yourself one who enjoys easy, normal, natural, and pleasing relationships with others.

I cannot urge you too strongly to consider the importance of this subject and to give time and attention to its mastery, for you will never be fully happy or successful until you do. Failure in this capacity will adversely affect you psychologically. To be liked is of profounder importance than mere ego satisfaction. As necessary as that is to your success in life, normal and satisfactory personal relations are even more important.

The feeling of not being wanted or needed is one of the most devastating of all human reactions. To the degree to which you are sought after or needed by other people will you become a fully-released person. The "lone wolf," the isolated personality, the retiring individual, these people suffer a misery which is difficult to describe. In self-defense they retire ever further within themselves. Their ingrowing, introverted nature is denied the normal development which the outgoing, self-giving person experiences. Unless the personality is drawn out of itself and can be of value to someone, it may sicken and die. The feeling of not being wanted or needed produces frustration, aging, illness. If you have a feeling of uselessness, if nobody needs or wants you, you really ought to do something about it. It is not only a pathetic way to live but is serious psychologically. Those who deal with the problems of human nature constantly encounter this problem and its unfortunate results.

Countless other people, not particularly victims of deep, unconscious psychological conflicts, have never mastered the knack of being popular. They try hard enough. They even go to extremes, often acting in a manner they do not really enjoy, but which they employ only because of their intense desire to have people like them. Everywhere today we see people putting on an act because of their inordinate desire for popularity in the superficial sense in which the word is often used in modern society.

The fact is that popularity can be attained by a few simple, natural, normal, and easily mastered techniques. Practice them diligently and you can become a well-liked person.

First, become a comfortable person, that is, one with whom people can associate without a sense of strain. Of some persons it is said, "You can never quite get next to him." There is always a barrier that you can't get over. A comfortable person is easy-going and natural. He has a pleasant, kindly, genial way about him. Being with him is not unlike wearing an old hat or an old pair of shoes, or an easy old coat. A stiff, reserved, unresponsive individual never meshes into the group. He is always just a bit out of it. You never quite know how to take him or how he will react. You just aren't easy-like with him.

Christianity teaches that one basic trait will go far toward getting people to like you. That trait is a sincere and forthright interest in and love for people. Perhaps if you cultivate this basic trait, other traits will naturally develop.

If you are not the comfortable type of person, I suggest that you make a study of your personality with a view toward eliminating conscious and unconscious elements of strain which may exist. Do not assume that the reason other people do not like you is because of something wrong with them. Assume, instead, that the trouble is within yourself and determine to find and eliminate it. This will require scrupulous honesty and it may also involve the assistance of personality experts. The so-called "scratchy" elements in your personality may be qualities which you have taken on through the years. Perhaps they have been assumed defensively, or they may be the result of attitudes developed in your younger days. Regardless of origin they can be eliminated by a scientific study of yourself and by your recognition of the necessity for change followed by a process of personality rehabilitation.

Essentially, getting people to like you is merely the other side of liking them. One of the most popular men who lived in the United States within the lifetime of most of us was the late Will Rogers. One of the most characteristic statements he ever made was, "I never met a man I didn't like." That may have been a slight exaggeration, but I am sure Will Rogers did not regard it as such. That is the way he felt about people, and as a result people opened up to him like flowers to the sun.

Sometimes the weak objection is offered that it is difficult to like some people. Granted, some people are by nature more likable than others, nevertheless a serious attempt to know any individual will reveal qualities within him that are admirable, even lovable.

A man had the problem of conquering feelings of irritation toward persons with whom he was associated. For some people he had a very profound dislike. They irritated him intensely, but he conquered these feelings simply by making an exhaustive list of everything he could possibly admire about each person who annoyed him. Daily he attempted to add to this list. He was surprised to discover that people whom he thought he did not like at all proved to have many pleasing qualities. In fact, he was at a loss to understand how he ever disliked them after becoming conscious of their attractive qualities. Of course, while he was making these discoveries about them, they, in turn, were finding new and likable qualities in him.

If you have gone through life up to this point without having established satisfactory human relationships, do not assume that you cannot change, but it will be necessary to take very definite steps toward solving the problem. You can change and become a popular person, well liked and esteemed, if you are willing to make the effort. May I remind you as I remind myself that one of the greatest tragedies of the average person is the tendency to spend our whole lives perfecting our faults? We develop a fault and we nurse it and cultivate it, and never change it. Like a needle caught in the groove of a defective record on a victrola, it plays the same old tune over and over again. You must lift the needle out of the groove, then you will have disharmony no longer, but harmony. Don't spend more of your life perfecting faults in human relations. Spend the rest of your life perfecting your great capacities for friendliness, for personal relations are vitally important to successful living.

Still another important factor in getting people to like you is to practice building up the ego of other persons. The ego, being the essence of our personalities, is sacred to us. There is in every person a normal desire for a feeling of self-importance. If I deflate your ego and therefore your self-importance, though you may laugh it off, I have deeply wounded you. In fact, I have shown disrespect for you, and while you may exercise charity toward me, even so, unless you are finely developed spiritually, you are not going to like me very well.

On the other hand, if I elevate your self-respect and contribute to your feeling of personal worth, I am showing high esteem for your ego. I have helped you to be your best self and therefore you appreciate what I have done. You are grateful to me. You like me for it.

The deflation of another person's ego may be mildly done perhaps, but one can never evaluate how deep the depreciation goes from even a remark or an attitude that is not meant to be unkind. Here is the way in which ego is often deflated.

The next time you are in a group and someone tells a joke and everybody laughs with appreciation and pleasure except yourself, when the laughter has died down say patronizingly, "Well, that is a pretty good joke all right. I saw it in a magazine last month."

Of course it will make you feel quite important to let others know of your superior knowledge, but how does it make the man feel who told the joke? You have robbed him of the satisfaction of having told a good story. You have crowded him out of his brief moment in the limelight and usurped attention to yourself. In fact you have taken the wind out of his sails and left him flat and deflated. He enjoyed his momentary little prominence, but you took it away from him. Nobody in that group is going to like you for what you did, and certainly not the man whose story you spoiled. Whether you like the joke or not, let the storyteller and the others enjoy it. Remember he may be a little bit embarassed and shy. It would have done him good to have received a response. Don't deflate people. Build them up and they will love you for it.

Whomever you help to build up and become a better, stronger, finer person will give you his undying devotion. Build up as many people as you can. Do it unselfishly. Do it because you like them and because you see possibilities in them. Do this and you will never lack for friends. You will always be well thought of. Build people up and love them geniunely. Do them good and their esteem and affection will flow back toward you.

The basic principles of getting people to like you need no prolonged and labored emphasis, for they are very simple and easily illustrate their own truth. However, I list ten practical rules for getting the esteem of others. The soundness of these principles has been demonstrated innumerable times. Practice them until you become expert at them and people will like you.

❖**1.** Learn to remember names. Inefficiency at this point may indicate that your interest is not sufficiently outgoing. A man's name is very important to him.

❖**2.** Be a comfortable person so there is no strain in being with you — be an old-shoe, old-hat kind of individual. Be homey.

❖**3.** Acquire the quality of relaxed easy-goingness so that things do not ruffle you.

❖**4.** Don't be egotistical. Guard against giving the impression that you know it all. Be natural and normally humble.

❖**5.** Cultivate the quality of being interesting so that people will want to be with you and get something of stimulating value from their association with you.

❖**6.** Study to get the "scratchy" elements out of your personality, even those of which you may be unconscious.

❖**7.** Sincerely attempt to heal, on an honest Christian basis, every misunderstanding you have had or now have. Drain off your grievances.

❧ **8.** Practice liking people until you learn to do so genuinely. Remember what Will Rogers said, "I never met a man I didn't like." Try to be that way.

❧ **9.** Never miss an opportunity to say a word of congratulation upon anyone's achievement, or express sympathy in sorrow or disappointment.

❧ **10.** Get a deep spiritual experience so that you have something to give people that will help them to be stronger and meet life more effectively. Give strength to people and they will give affection to you.

❊(16)❊

Prescription For Heartache

"Please give me a prescription for heartache."

This curious and rather pathetic request was made by a man who had been informed by his doctor that the feelings of disability of which he complained were not of a physical nature. His trouble lay in an inability to rise above sorrow. He was suffering from "an ache in his personality" as a result of grief.

His doctor advised him to secure spiritual consultation and treatment. So continuing to use the terminology of medicine, he repeated his question, "Is there a spiritual prescription which will reduce my constant inner suffering? I realize that sorrow comes to everyone and I should be able to meet it the same as others. I have tried my best but find no peace." Again he asked with a sad, slow smile, "Give me a prescription for heartache."

There is indeed a "prescription" for heartache. One element in the prescription is physical activity. The sufferer must avoid the temptation to sit and brood. A sensible program which substitutes physical activity for such fruitless brooding reduces the strain on the area of the mind where we reflect, philosophize, and suffer mental pain. Muscular activity utilizes another part of the brain and therefore shifts the strain and gives relief.

An old country lawyer who had a sound philosophy and much wisdom told a sorrowing woman that the best medicine for a broken heart is "to take a scrubbing brush and get down on your knees and go to work. The best medicine for a man," he declared, "is to get an ax and chop wood until physically tired." While this is not guaranteed to be a complete cure for heartache, yet it does tend to mitigate such suffering.

Whatever the character of your heartache, one of the first steps is to resolve to escape from any defeatist situation which may have been created around yourself, even though it is difficult to do so, and return once again to the normal course of your life. Get back into the main stream of life's activities. Take up your old associations. Form new ones. Get busy walking, riding, swimming, playing — get the blood to coursing through your system. Lose yourself in some worth-while project. Fill your days with creative activity and emphasize the physical aspect of activity. Employ healthy mind-relieving busyness, but be sure that it is of a worth-while and constructive nature. Superficial escapism through feverish activity merely deadens pain temporarily and does not heal, as, for example, parties and drinking.

An excellent and normal release from heartache is to give way to grief. There is a foolish point of view current today that one should not show grief, that it is not proper to cry or express oneself through the natural mechanism of tears and sobbing. This is a denial of the law of nature. It is natural to cry when pain or sorrow comes. It is a relief mechanism provided in the body by Almighty God and should be used.

To restrain grief, to inhibit it, to bottle it up, is to fail to use one of God's means for eliminating the pressure of sorrow. Like every other function of the human body and nervous system, this must be controlled, but it should not be denied altogether. A good cry by either man or woman is a release from heartache. I should warn, however, that this mechanism should not be used unduly nor allowed to become a habitual process. Should that happen, it partakes of the nature of abnormal grief and could become a psychosis. Unrestraint of any kind should not be allowed.

I receive many letters from people whose loved ones have died. They tell me that it is very difficult for them to go to the same places they were in the habit of frequenting together or to be with the same people with whom they associated as a couple or as a family. Therefore they avoid the old-time places and friends.

I regard this as a serious mistake. A secret of curing heartache is to be as normal and natural as possible. This does not imply disloyalty or indifference. This policy is important in avoiding a state of abnormal grief. Normal sorrow is a natural process and its normality is evidenced by the ability of the individual to return to his usual pursuits and responsibilities and continue therein as formerly.

The deeper remedy for heartache, of course, is the curative comfort supplied by trust in God. Inevitably the basic prescription for heartache is to turn to God in an attitude of faith and empty the mind and heart to Him. Perseverance in the act of spiritual self-emptying will finally bring healing to the broken heart. This generation, which has suffered fully as much if not more heartache than people in preceding eras, needs to relearn that which the wisest men of all time have known, namely, that there is no healing of the pain suffered by humanity except through the benign ministrations of faith.

One of the greatest souls of the ages was Brother Lawrence, who said, "If in this life we would know the serene peace of Paradise, we must school ourselves in familiar, humble, and loving converse with God." It is not advisable to attempt to carry the burden of sorrow and mental pain without Divine help, for its weight is more than the personality can bear. The simplest and most effective of all prescriptions for heartache then is to practice the presence of God. This will soothe the ache in your heart and ultimately heal the wound. Men and women who have experienced great tragedy tell us that this prescription is effective.

Another profoundly curative element in the prescription for heartache is to gain a sound and satifying philosophy of life and death and deathlessness. For my part, when I gained the unshakable belief that there is no death, that all life is indivisible, that the here and hereafter are one, that time and eternity are inseparable, that this is one unobstructed universe, then I found the most satisfying and convincing philosophy of my entire life.

These convictions are based upon sound foundations, the Bible for one. I believe that the Bible gives us a very subtle, and as will be proved ultimately, a scientific series of insights into the great question, "What happens when a man leaves this world?" Also the Bible very wisely tells us that we know these truths by faith. Henri Bergson, the philosopher, says that the surest way into truth is by perception, by intuition, by reasoning to a certain point, then by taking a "mortal leap," and by intuition attaining the truth. You come to some glorious moment where you simply "know." That is the way it happened to me.

I am absolutely, wholeheartedly, and thoroughly convinced of the truth of which I write and have no doubt of it, even to an infinitesimal degree. I arrived at this positive faith gradually, yet there came one moment when I knew.

This philosophy will not ward off the sorrow which comes when a loved one dies and physical, earthly separation ensues. But it will lift and dissipate grief. It will fill your mind with a deep understanding of the meaning of this inevitable circumstance. And it will give you a deep assurance that you have not lost your loved one. Live on this faith and you will be at peace and the ache will leave your heart.

Take into your mind and heart one of the most marvelous texts in the Holy Bible — "Eye hath not seen, nor ear heard, neither have entered into the heart of man, the things which God hath prepared for them that love Him." (I Corinthians 2:9)

This means that you have never seen, no matter what you have seen, however wonderful it is, you have never seen anything to compare with the marvelous things that God has prepared for those who love Him and who put their trust in Him. Moreover, it says that you have never heard anything to compare with the astonishing marvels that God has laid up for those who follow His teachings and live according to His spirit. Not only have you never seen nor ever heard but you have never even dimly imagined what He is going to do for you. This sentence goes all out in promising comfort and immortality and reunion and every good thing to those who center their lives in God.

After many years of reading the Bible and being intimately connected with all the phases of the lives of hundreds of people, I wish to state unequivocally that I have found this Biblical promise to be absolutely true. It applies even to this world. People who really practice living on a Christlike basis have the most incredible things happen to them.

This passage also relates to the state of existence of those now living on the other side and our relationship, while we live, to those who have preceded us across that barrier which we call death. I use the word "barrier" somewhat apologetically. We have always thought of death as a barrier with a concept of a separatist nature.

Scientists working today in the field of parapsychology and extra-sensory perception and experimenting in precognition, telepathy, clairvoyance (all of which were formerly considered paraphernalia of the cranks, but which are now of sound, scientific usage in the laboratories), are expressing themselves as believing that the soul survives the barrier of time and space. In effect, we are on the edge of one of the greatest scientific discoveries in history which will substantiate, on a laboratory-exploratory basis, the existence of the soul and its deathlessness.

For many years I have been accumulating a series of incidents, the validity of which I accept and which bear out the conviction that we live in a dynamic universe where life, not death, is the basic principle. I have confidence in the people who have described their experiences and am convinced that they indicate a world impinged upon or intertwined with our own through the meshes of which human spirits, on both sides of death, live in unbroken fellowship. The conditions of life on the other side, as we know them in mortality, are modified. Undoubtedly those who have crossed to the other side dwell in a higher medium than we do and their understanding is amplified beyond ours, yet all the facts point to the continued existence of our loved ones and the further fact that they are not far away, and still another fact implied, but no less real, that we shall be reunited with them. Meanwhile, we continue in fellowship with those who dwell in the spirit world.

The New Testament teaches the indestructibility of life in a most interesting and simple manner. It describes Jesus after His crucifixion in a series of appearances, disappearances, and reappearances. Some saw Him and then He vanished out of their sight. Then others saw Him and again He vanished. It is as if to say, "You see me and then you do not see me." This indicates that He is trying to tell us that when we do not see Him, it does not mean He is not there. Out of sight does not mean out of life. Occasional mystical appearances which some experience indicate the same truth, that He is near by. Did He not say, ". . . because I live, ye shall live also." (John 14:19) In other words, our loved ones who have died in this faith are also near by and occasionally draw near to comfort us.

Of these deep and tender matters I personally have no doubt whatsoever. I firmly believe in the continuation of life after that which we call death takes place. I believe there are two sides to the phenomenon known as death — this side where we now live and the other side where we shall continue to live. Eternity does not start with death. We are in eternity now. We are citizens of eternity. We merely change the form of the experience called life, and that change, I am persuaded, is for the better.

My mother was a great soul, and her influence on me will ever stand out in my life as an experience that cannot be surpassed. She was a wonderful conversationalist. Her mind was keen and alert. She traveled the world over and enjoyed wide contacts as a Christian leader in missionary causes. Her life was full and rich. She had a marvelous sense of humor. She was good company, and I always loved to be with her. She was considered by all who knew her an unusually fascinating and stimulating personality.

During my adult years whenever I had the opportunity I would go home to see her. I always anticipated the arrival at the family home, for it was an exciting experience in which everyone talked at once as we sat around the breakfast table. What happy reunions — what glorious meetings. Then came her death, and we tenderly laid her body in the beautiful little cemetery at Lynchburg in southern Ohio, a town where she had lived as a girl. I was very sad the day we left her there, and went away heavy-hearted. It was in the fullness of summertime when we took her home to her last resting place.

It came autumn, and I felt that I wanted to be with my mother again. I was lonely without her, therefore I decided to go to Lynchburg. All night long on the train I thought sadly of the happy days now gone and how things were utterly changed and would never be the same again.

So I came to the little town. The weather was cold and the sky overcast as I walked to the cemetery. I pushed through the old iron gates and my feet rustled in the leaves as I walked to her grave where I sat sad and lonely. Of a sudden the clouds parted and the sun came through. It lighted up the Ohio hills in gorgeous autumn colors, the hills where I grew up as a boy, which I have always loved so well, where she herself had played as a girl in the long ago.

Then all of a sudden I seemed to hear her voice. Now I didn't actually hear her voice, but I seemed to. I am sure I heard it by the inward ear. The message was clear and distinct. It was stated in her beloved old-time tone, and this is what she said, "Why seek ye the living among the dead? I am not here. Do you think that I would stay in this dark and dismal place? I am with you and my loved ones always." In a burst of inner light I became wondrously happy. I knew that what I had heard was the truth. The message came to me with all the force of actuality. I could have shouted, and I stood up and put my hand on the tombstone and saw it for what it is, only a place where mortal remains lay. The body was there, to be sure, but it was only a coat that had been laid off because the wearer needed it no longer. But she, that gloriously lovely spirit, she was not there.

I walked out of that place and only rarely since have I returned. I like to go back there and think of her and the old days of my youth, but no longer is it a place of gloom. It is merely a symbol, for she is not there. She is with us her loved ones. "Why seek ye the living among the dead?" (Luke 24:5)

Read and believe the Bible as it tells about the goodness of God and the immortality of the soul. Pray sincerely and with faith. Make prayer and faith the habit of your life. Learn to have real fellowship with God and with Jesus Christ. As you do this you will find a deep conviction welling up in your mind that these wonderful things are true indeed.

". . . if it were not so, I would have told you." (John 14:2) You can depend upon the reliability of Christ. He would not let you believe and hold convictions so sacred in nature unless they are absolutely true.

So in this faith, which is a sound, substantial, and rational view of life and eternity, you have the prescription for heartache.

❊(17)❊

How To Draw Upon That Higher Power

 When quite young I was called to a large church in a university community and many of my congregation were professors in the university as well as leading citizens of the city. I wanted to justify the confidence of those who gave me such an outstanding opportunity and accordingly worked very hard. As a result I began to experience overstrain. Everyone should work hard, but there is no virtue in overtrying or overpressing to such an extent that you do not work efficiently. It is somewhat like making a golf shot. Try to "kill" the ball and you execute the shot poorly. You can do likewise in your job. I began to get rather tired and nervous and had no feeling of normal power.

One day I decided to call on one of the professors, the late Hugh M. Tilroe, a great friend of mine. He was a wonderful teacher, and he was also a great fisherman and hunter. He was a man's man, an outdoor personality. I knew that if I did not find him at the university he would be out on the lake fishing, and sure enough there he was. He came ashore at my hail. "The fish are biting — come on," he said. I climbed in his boat and we fished awhile.

"What's the matter, son?" he asked with understanding. I told him how hard I was trying and that it was getting me down nervously. "I have no feeling of lift or power," I said.

He chuckled. "Maybe you're trying too hard."

As the boat scraped the shore he said, "Come in the house with me." As we entered his cabin he ordered, "Lie down there on that couch. I want to read you something. Shut your eyes and relax while I find the quotation."

I did as directed, and thought he was going to read me some philosophical or perhaps diverting piece, but instead he said, "Here it is. Listen quietly while I read it to you. And let these words sink in. 'Hast thou not known? Hast thou not heard, that the everlasting God, the Lord, the Creator of the ends of the earth, fainteth not, neither is weary? There is no searching of his understanding. He giveth power to the faint; and to them that have no might he increaseth strength. Even the youths shall faint and be weary, and the young men shall utterly fall. But they that wait upon the Lord shall renew their strength; they shall mount up with wings as eagles; they shall run, and not be weary; and they shall walk, and not faint.' " (Isaiah 40:28-31) Then he asked, "Do you know from what I am reading?"

"Yes, the fortieth chapter of Isaiah," I answered.

"I'm glad you know your Bible," he commented. "Why don't you practice it? Now relax. Take three deep breaths — in and out slowly. Practice resting yourself in God. Practice depending upon Him for His support and power. Believe He is giving it to you now and don't get out of touch with that power. Yield yourself to it — let it flow through you.

"Give your job all you've got. Of course you must do that. But do it in a relaxed and easy manner like a batter in a big-league ball game. He swings the bat easy-like, and doesn't try to knock the ball out of the park. He just does the best he can and believes in himself because he knows that he has lots of reserve power." Then he repeated the passage again. " 'They that wait upon the Lord shall renew their strength.' "

That was a long time ago, but I never forgot that lesson. He taught me how to draw upon that Higher Power, and believe me, his suggestions worked. I continue to follow my friend's advice, and it has never failed me in the more than twenty years that have passed since then. My life is crowded with activity but that power formula gives me all the strength I need.

A second method for drawing upon that Higher Power is to learn to take a positive, optimistic attitude toward every problem. In direct proportion to the intensity of the faith which you muster will you receive power to meet your situations. "According to your faith be it unto you," (Matthew 9:29) is a basic law of successful living.

There is a Higher Power, and that Power can do everything for you. Draw upon it and experience its great helpfulness. Why be defeated when you are free to draw upon that Higher Power? State your problem. Ask for a specific answer. Believe that you are getting that answer. Believe that now, through God's help, you are gaining power over your difficulty.

This Higher Power is one of the most amazing facts in human existence. I am awestruck, no matter how many times I have seen the phenomenon, by the thorough-going, tremendous, overwhelming changes for good that it accomplishes in the lives of people. Personally, I am so enthusiastic about all that the Higher Power can do for people that I am loath to bring this book to a close. I could recite story after story, incident after incident of those who by laying hold of this power have had a new birth of life.

This power is constantly available. If you open to it, it will rush in like a mighty tide. It is there for anybody under any circumstances or in any condition. This tremendous inflow of power is of such force that in its inrush it drives everything before it, casting out fear, hate, sickness, weakness, moral defeat, scattering them as though they had never touched you, refreshing and restrengthening your life with health, happiness, and goodness.

Why not draw upon that Higher Power?

Epilogue

You have finished this book. What have you read?

Simply a series of practical and workable techniques for living a successful life. You have read a formula of belief and practice which should help you win victory over every defeat.

But reading is not enough. Now please go back and persistently practice each technique given in this book. Keep at it until you obtain the desired results.

I wrote this book out of a sincere desire to help you. It will give me great happiness to know that the book has helped you. I have absolute confidence and belief in the principles and methods outlined in this volume. They have been tested in the laboratory of spiritual experience and practical demonstration. They work when worked.

We may never meet in person, but in this book we have met. We are spiritual friends. I pray for you. God will help you — so believe and live successfully.

NORMAN VINCENT PEALE